Future of Business and Finance

The Future of Business and Finance book series features professional works aimed at defining, analyzing, and charting the future trends in these fields. The focus is mainly on strategic directions, technological advances, challenges and solutions which may affect the way we do business tomorrow, including the future of sustainability and governance practices. Mainly written by practitioners, consultants and academic thinkers, the books are intended to spark and inform further discussions and developments.

Angelo Rosa

New Business Organizational Models for Governing in Times of Change

From Classical HR Models to the Role of AI

Springer

Angelo Rosa
Department of Management, Finance and Technology
University LUM Giuseppe Degennaro
Casamassima, Bari, Italy

ISSN 2662-2467 ISSN 2662-2475 (electronic)
Future of Business and Finance
ISBN 978-3-032-04090-9 ISBN 978-3-032-04091-6 (eBook)
https://doi.org/10.1007/978-3-032-04091-6

This Springer imprint is published by the registered company Springer Nature Switzerland AG
The registered company address is: Gewerbestrasse 11, 6330 Cham, Switzerland

About the Book

In a world where incremental headways are insufficient to address the multifaceted challenges posed by a VUCA environment, organizations require a re-evaluation of their classical governing models. The idea of governing in change demonstrates the capacity to lead and adapt in the midst of turbulent situations. This monograph argues that "governing in change" is of vital significance. While "governing change" infers a focus on overseeing particular alteration activities, "governing in change" speaks to a more all-encompassing approach that manages changes as a crucial aspect of organizational elements and underscores the requirement for organizations to continuously adapt and evolve their governing structure in response to the complexities of the advanced commerce environment. This monograph aims to explore the critical evolution of organizational governance and the shift from classical HR models to innovative AI-driven organizational models to navigate the turbulent changes in a VUCA environment. In this regard, the monograph focuses on identifying the emerging organizational models that reflect the move toward "governing in change" with a specific focus on the AI integration in governance structures. To address this aim, and while the existing literature concentrates mainly on the advantages of AI in HR, but it does not fully take into account the larger implications on governance structures, cultural changes, and ethics. This monograph also adopts a systematic literature review according to the PRISMA Methodology (Moher et al., 2009) and the Affinity Approach (Islam, 2005; Iqbal et al., 2022) in order to enrich the analysis and synthesis of the insights of the final selected 93 articles. The results demonstrate seven new organizational models with employee-centered practices, agility, digitalization, AI-led leadership, data-informed decision-making, cultural change, and sustainability, which reflect organizational governance in change. Indeed, emerging organizational models represent a paradigm shift from classical models to the adoption of new paradigms, with AI being a primary driving force in change management. This monograph offers relevant theoretical and managerial implications. On the theoretical level, it addresses five significant research gaps as below: (1) Lack of understanding of the AI role and its direct connection to change management procedures and governance structures. According to the findings, AI as a pivotal tool in governing in change facilitates change management through promoting personalized learning, communication via chatbots, real-time data utilization, and AI-optimized organizational performance. (2) Addressing a lack of understanding regarding how HR and AI systems can effectively synergize.

Findings on "AI-Driven Career Development" openly address human–AI interaction, stressing the necessity to redefine the job and encourage HR collaboration in change efforts. (3) Addressing the gap regarding how AI can transform human-centered design (HCD) principles and strategic HR partnerships. Findings offer AI to enable personalized plans for HR and AI crafting to facilitate more effective HR redesign practices. (4) Addressing the lack of industry-specific and customized organizational models. Providing models on "collaborative leadership models," "agility and adaptability," and "cultural change" by creating organization-specific models across industries. (5) The necessity for normative and robust frameworks for principles-based, ethical, responsible, and sustainable AI governance. By indicating frameworks promoting transparency, fairness, and accountability.

Contents

List of Figures

List of Tables

Introduction

1

Abstract

This monograph investigates the changing landscape of organizational governance in the VUCA world with a focus on the inability of old bureaucratic and Taylorist models to capture the complexities of today. It discusses how advancements in artificial intelligence (AI) are resetting governance architecture, leadership profiles, and human resource management, enabling agility, resilience, and foresight-oriented change management. Through a systematic literature review based on the PRISMA protocol and Affinity Approach, the study synthesizes 94 studies in order to reveal new organizational designs for ethical and responsible AI integration. Major contributions include describing how AI facilitates individualized learning, strategic decision-making, and HR reform; setting up sector-specific governance frameworks; and highlighting the use of ethical principles like fairness and transparency. This monograph promotes moving from change management to leadership for change, centering on adaptive leadership, people-first, and ethical AI integration to better propel digital transformation. The extensive critique offers practice and policy advice along with case studies of HR innovations based on AI. The book overall is a good beginning to read about adaptive, people-centric governance models that can endure the age of swift technological and environmental change.

In the age of the VUCA world, the times of uncertainty, complexity, volatility, and ambiguity, organizational governance systems and their management practices continue to be strained to keep up with the dynamism of ever-changing environments (Taskan et al., 2022).

A. Rosa, *New Business Organizational Models for Governing in Times of Change*, Future of Business and Finance,
https://doi.org/10.1007/978-3-032-04091-6_1

There is agreement that VUCA conditions are difficult times for leaders to confront. The unpredictability of times and the difficulty of understanding technological advancements that impact industry, as well as the consequences of demographic shifts in the workforce, render any efforts to understand the future and to prepare responses (Bennett & Lemoine, 2014). Technological advancements will transform the future HR organization structure (DiRomualdo et al., 2018). Douglas and Haley (2025) suggest that HR leaders, in order to adapt to dynamic market conditions and future readiness, consider a comprehensive redesign of organizational structures and heighten HR's role as a strategic partner.

In such a situation, bureaucratic and Taylorist assumptions, and the classical models, with the focus on predictability, control, and hierarchy, are considered today inadequate to match the complexity of the contemporary business environment and are unable to effectively tackle the dynamic complexities of contemporary organizations (Atanassova et al., 2025).

Therefore, it is argued that amid ongoing change, novel leadership styles and innovative technological advances are necessary to succeed. The adoption and implementation of AI, conversely to inflexible, control-focused mechanisms, are revolutionizing organizational operational and governance dynamics (Joseph & Sengul, 2025) and allowing organizations to make more participatory, agile, and information-based governance models possible (Rudko et al., 2024). Meanwhile, a novel leadership style enhances adaptability skills and agility in organizations.

As indicated by Kaur et al. (2021), the adoption of AI technologies has a revolutionary impact on human resource management. While current literature recognizes the potential of AI for transformation, especially in the HR domain, there are significant gaps in how these technologies influence change management procedures, governance systems, and organizational culture directly (Jatobá et al., 2023).

In addition, most of the recent researches make general conclusions without enough evidence to accept industry-level issues or advanced human–AI interaction to enable beneficial realization (Jatobá et al., 2023). Besides that, the hasty embracing of AI also poses ethical, social, and strategic dangers that must be stopped with utmost caution. Algorithmic bias, privacy of data, decision transparency, and disqualification of human skill set are all concerns for using AI responsibly (Papagiannidis et al., 2025; Singhraul & Anuragi, 2024). In spite of the technology's potential, organizations are beset by suspicion and doubt about the ethics and future viability of AI (Kolbjørnsrud et al., 2017).

Furthermore, AI integration contradicts traditional HR and organizational paradigms, which require more agile, HR-oriented, and ethical governance systems. This monograph uses a systematic literature review methodology followed by the PRISMA protocol (Moher et al., 2009) to address these research gaps and to seek an answer to this research question: *What are the emerging organizational models for governing in change, focusing on transitioning from classical HR models to integrating artificial intelligence (AI)?*

To improve the analysis's depth and granularity and to compile the results of 93 carefully chosen research studies that examine the relationship between corporate governance, HR procedures, and AI technologies, the Affinity Approach (Islam,

2005; Iqbal et al., 2022) was employed. The key goal is to create a deeper insight into how organizations can move from traditional HR paradigms toward proactive, AI-based systems of governance that are best placed to manage change responsibly and successfully.

The idea of governing in change and the necessity of adaptation typify the capacity to lead and adjust in the midst of turbulent situations and encourage a proactive reaction to outside pressures.

This monograph argues that "governing in change," characterized by flexible leadership, employee-centric models, and moral AI integration, is of vital significance, especially as organizations explore the complexities brought by AI and other digital innovations. Indeed, the integration of AI's potential to address the complexities of the present-day UVCA environment requires a move from simply managing change to proactively governing within it.

While "governing change" infers a focus on overseeing particular alteration activities, "governing in change" speaks to a more all-encompassing approach that coordinates changes as a crucial aspect of organizational elements and underscores the requirement for organizations to advance their management systems in response to the complexities of the advanced commerce environment. Organizations require a re-evaluation of conventional governing models.

Eventually, this study contributes to theoretical and practical discussion around the creation of resilient, flexible organizations more likely to succeed in the midst of prevailing technological and environmental dynamism.

This monograph offers relevant theoretical and managerial implications. On the theoretical level, it addresses five significant research gaps as below:

1. Lack of understanding of the AI role and its direct connection to change management procedures and governance structures. According to the findings, AI as a pivotal tool in governing in change facilitates change management through promoting personalized learning, communication via chatbots, real-time data utilization, and AI-optimized organizational performance.
2. Addressing a lack of understanding regarding how HR and AI systems can effectively synergize. Findings on "AI-Driven Career Development" openly address human–AI interaction, stressing the necessity to redefine the job and encourage HR collaboration in change efforts.
3. Addressing the gap regarding how AI can transform human-centered design (HCD) principles and strategic HR partnerships. Findings offer AI to enable personalized plans for HR and AI crafting to facilitate more effective HR redesign practices.
4. Addressing the lack of industry-specific and customized organizational models. Providing models on "collaborative leadership models," "agility and adaptability," and "cultural change" by creating organization-specific models across industries.
5. The necessity is for normative and robust frameworks for principles-based, ethical, responsible, and sustainable AI governance, which promote transparency, fairness, and accountability.

Hence, this monograph, in a solid, multifaceted way, establishes a structured understanding of the OR–AI nexus and emerging patterns in the examined topics, lays a foundation for practical and human-centered organizational models that are adaptable to turbulent environments, and offers a new perspective on the AI role not only as a tool for automation and enhanced efficiency but also as a central driver shaping organizational structure, leadership, and HR.

The structure of this monograph is arranged as follows: The introductory chapters (Chaps. 1 and 2) lay the foundation by presenting the main concepts and offering an extensive explanation of AI applications in human resources.

Chapter 1 provides context: Why new organizational models are needed in an ever-changing world. Chapter 2 looks more closely at the specific technologies of AI, the impact on work organizations, and how this technology makes it possible to think in a new way about roles, tasks, and skills. This section not only explains the technological scene but also explicates the advantages, challenges, and ethical considerations, serving as a solid foundation for the remaining part of the study.

Chapters 3 and 4 look at how governance and leadership are changing on the foundation of this technological vision. By contrast, Chapter 3 stresses the evolution of governance from a reactive to a proactive control, agile and strategic responses, including AI-based decision-making and ethical control.

Chapter 4 looks at leadership, encouraging human–AI collaboration, ethical rectitude, and transformational leadership needed in the new landscape of AI usage. Adding insight and rigor through the inclusion of Chap. 5, Research Methodology and Materials, which documents research design and systematic literature review (SLR), this monograph integrates scholarly accuracy to front-run themes such as organizational transformation, AI-based decision-making, ethical governance, and HR transformation based on empirical facts and projecting dominant trends and lacunae. Chapters 6 and 7 then shift to Discussion and Theoretical Considerations.

Chapter 6 pulls together the findings and presents new organizational forms that embody governance in transition. It discusses how AI-led HR transformation would result in employee-centric governance, heightened agility, data-powered practices, and ethical AI governance. The chapter discusses the practical implications of these shifts, including flexible structures, holacracy, and digital and their impact on leadership and culture.

Chapter 7 further develops the theoretical debate by comparing governing change to governing in change. It highlights the role of AI in supporting this transformation, in particular in disruptive contexts, and the ethical issues that must be addressed for responsible governance. Chapter 8 provides recommendations for policy-makers, managing bodies, and practitioners toward supportive policies, infrastructure investments, industry-based AI strategies, and further research. It emphasizes the need for extended collaborative work to integrate AI in an ethical and effective way inside organizational boundaries.

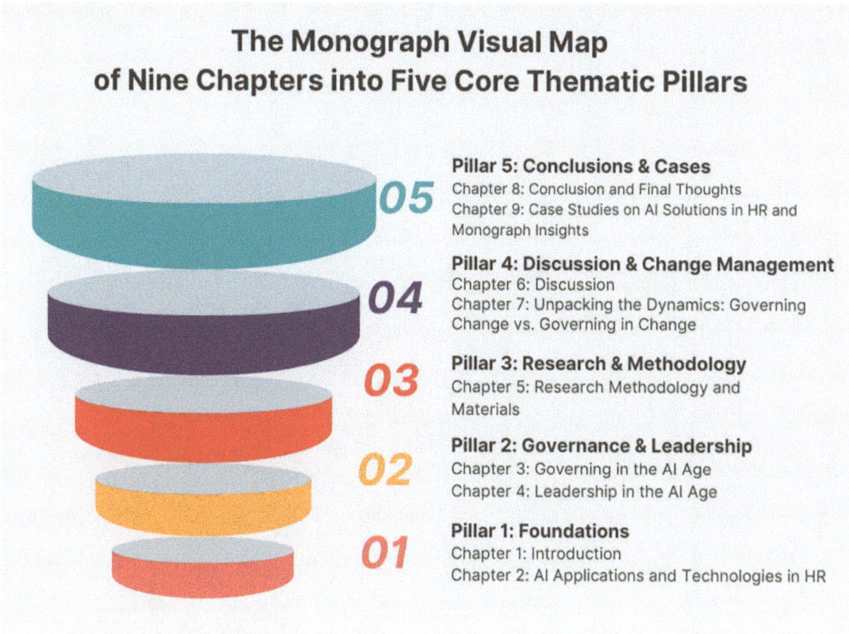

Fig. 1.1 This 'monograph's visual map

Chapter 9 offers practical applications, examples, and case studies of AI in HR, illustrating how companies transform HR, align with strategic goals, and foster positive changes in culture and ethics. These cases serve as practical exemplars linking theory and practice and building on the book's key concepts. Figure 1.1 shows this monograph's chapter organization graphical map.

2 AI Applications and Technologies in HR

Abstract

The different applications and implications of artificial intelligence (AI) in human resources (HR) as a driver of organizational change and a counterpoint to automation are discussed in this chapter. Artificial intelligence technologies such as computer vision, natural language processing, machine learning, and generative AI are classified into cognitive insights, process automation, and cognitive engagement, which enable organizations to make more intelligent decisions, automate, and drive innovation at greater speeds. AI assumes responsibility for work arrangements and labor markets to a large degree, hence necessitating role reevaluation, promoting human–AI collaboration, and necessitating reskilling and upskilling initiatives in a bid to balance job replacement and skill obsolescence. Effective application of AI is based on culture of an organization, employee attitude, and ethical management with a focus on trust, transparency, and wise utilization. Advantages of AI in HR are enhanced efficiency, strategic talent management, individualized development, data-driven decision-making, and the added benefit of enabling agility and innovation. Generative AI offers paradigm-shifting opportunities of content generation, talent attraction, and reengineering organizations but has the disadvantage of risks such as ethics concerns, exacerbation of inequality, and erosion of skills. Understanding such complexities requires having master plans that bring technological innovation in conjunction with ethics to the level where AI becomes an enabler of sustainable organizational development and human-centric work culture during the technology era.

A. Rosa, *New Business Organizational Models for Governing in Times of Change*, Future of Business and Finance,
https://doi.org/10.1007/978-3-032-04091-6_2

The AI technologies and applications include machine learning, robotics, computer vision, and natural language processing, which are employed in many applications, from advanced prediction models and segmented marketing campaigns to customer service bots. The revolutionary impact AI offers allows organizations to improve customer relations, streamline procedures, gain a competitive advantage in a constantly evolving marketplace, and secure a strategic advantage (Gursoy & Cai, 2025).

The AI technologies are commonly classified into three categories: cognitive insights, process automation, and cognitive engagement (Ali Mohamad et al., 2023; Pillai & Sivathanu, 2020).

Cognitive insights examine large datasets using machine learning algorithms to produce useful information that helps with decision-making. Cognitive engagement includes interactive AI tools that improve employee engagement and customer service, such as chatbots. From process streamlining and enhancing existing goods and services to formulating new goods and services and aiding decision-making, all these technologies are utilized for various organizational activities (Benbya et al., 2020).

Also, by adopting sophisticated AI technologies, including natural language processing and machine learning, organizations may facilitate large-scale analytics, promote innovation, and align resource usage (Papagiannidis et al., 2025). Organizations need to acquire a comprehensive understanding of these technologies' strengths and weaknesses for effective implementation, ensuring that AI aligns with the organization's strategic business goals (Gursoy & Cai, 2025).

2.1 The AI Implications on HR Markets and Work Structures

The deep transformation of work nature is reflected in AI-facilitated organizational change, for which individual work practice realignment and traditional organizational structure must be called for (Benbya et al., 2020; Elkahlout et al., 2024). Implementation of AI technology becomes a key driver for decision-making, process innovation, and efficiency as companies wrestle with the intricacy of a VUCA environment (Gendron et al., 2024).

According to Benbya et al. (2020), AI is one of the technologies that will most certainly disrupt enterprises and fundamentally alter how organizations function. However, there are five main areas of concern regarding AI in the workplace: the effects on the labor market, employee attitudes, perceptions of capabilities, human–AI collaboration, and AI as a control mechanism (Bankins et al., 2024).

This emphasizes the necessity of moral AI systems that are regarded as just and reliable. Furthermore, ethical governance is essential to prevent AI from being utilized as a weapon for overbearing control while preserving workers' autonomy (Bankins et al., 2024). Thus, in light of the above and a thorough understanding of the complex effects of AI, the necessity of a comprehensive strategy for governing in change is highlighted.

2.2 Reimagining Work

Understanding the dynamic and mutual shaping of human and machine in a work context is fundamental. This entails changing, adapting, and rearranging work procedures (John et al., 2024). As AI develops, a workforce that can collaborate with intelligent systems is needed, necessitating an emphasis on human–AI collaboration that improves creativity and decision-making (Bankins et al. 2024).

Gladden et al. (2022) investigate the historical relationship between AI technologies and human workers, following the development of AI as a possible supervisor to the computer as a tool in the workplace. It makes the case that businesses must take proactive measures to handle the benefits and problems posed by the growing integration of AI into managerial jobs.

The debate over automation and artificial intelligence is presented in a balanced manner.

It emphasizes the potential for job creation and the enhancement of human capacities while simultaneously recognizing the actual risk of job displacement and its possible negative effects.

AI and automation can promote HR skills, develop new abilities, and result in employment growth. Thus, adopting a novel strategy that emphasizes adaptation, education, and addressing the ethics of AI is necessary to effectively manage this technological upheaval.

However, according to the literature, while AI brings several advantages, artificial intelligence poses challenges to employment stability and skill obsolescence; thus, negative perspectives demonstrate that there is a substantial threat of job displacement and a discussion of the social consequences of displacement, including the mental health issue and effects on the community.

Therefore, the future nature of employment becomes crucial to evolving with a stronger focus on human–AI collaboration, reinventing job crafting, a shift in human skills toward intricate cognitive and emotional intelligence, and the requirement for new skills.

2.2.1 HR and AI Collaboration: What Are the Opportunities and Challenges?

The HR and AI collaboration is now a reality and has become achievable. The majority of cognitive jobs are currently enhanced by AI rather than replaced, opening the door to new roles and ways that humans and AI can work together. To fully benefit from AI, human–AI collaboration must be effective (Bankins et al., 2024). This necessitates a sophisticated comprehension of organizational, group, and individual elements.

Worker attitudes toward AI, job design, and AI qualities are critical at the individual level. Successful integration requires addressing staff concerns and cultivating favorable attitudes toward AI (Bankins et al., 2024).

In order to effectively implement AI in organizations, employee perceptions are crucial, and it calls for resolving these concerns regarding job security and skill obsolescence through open communication and reskilling programs and a focus on promoting human–AI partnership (Gursoy & Cai, 2025). In addition, according to Bankins et al. (2024), HR behavior, effective collaboration, and shared occupational identity are necessary to achieve the full benefits of AI in organizations, and employees interact with AI. Through virtual assistants and collaborative platforms, AI influences team dynamics and promotes new kinds of collaboration (Elkahlout et al., 2024).

At the organizational level, innovative and supportive organizational cultures are vital for advancing the usage of AI. Organizations must therefore create a setting where people and AI coexist peacefully while utilizing each other's distinct advantages (Simón et al., 2024). Interoperability, trust, and reciprocal knowledge acquisition are necessary for this (Simón et al., 2024). The significance of the human element in organizational transformation acknowledges that a thorough grasp of the human elements influencing organizational performance must go hand in hand with technology adaptation.

Integrating AI inside organizational systems has accelerated a transformative move within the elements of collaboration across different levels.

This advancement requires a comprehensive understanding of compelling collaboration, individual variables affecting interaction, and the overarching suggestions on employee morale and organizational culture.

Figure 2.1 illustrates the key aspects of human–AI collaboration in the age of AI in organizations.

1. *Human Element*: At long last, the human component remains a basic factor within the integration of AI into organizational settings. Understanding human factors, ranging from cognitive biases to emotional responses, is basic for the effective implementation of AI innovations. Organizations must prioritize human-centric approaches that recognize and adapt to these factors, subsequently guaranteeing that AI serves as an enabler instead of a spoiler of human potential.
2. *Effective Collaboration*: Effective collaboration is recognized as a foundation of organizational success, especially within the setting of AI integration. As per Bankins et al. (2024), the collaborations should be at all levels, i.e., individual, group, and organizational. This multi-layered approach builds up so that HR and AI professionals work together harmoniously, enhancing efficiency and growth. Effective collaboration, not as it were, encourages the consistent exchange of thoughts and data, but moreover harnesses the complementary qualities of human inventiveness and machine effectiveness.
3. *Individual Factors*: The transaction between person components and AI interaction is essential for cultivating positive work environment situations. As highlighted by Bankins et al. (2024), positive states of mind and attitudes toward AI, astute work plan, and the inalienable qualities of the AI instruments themselves essentially impact person encounters. Employees who have a favorable view-

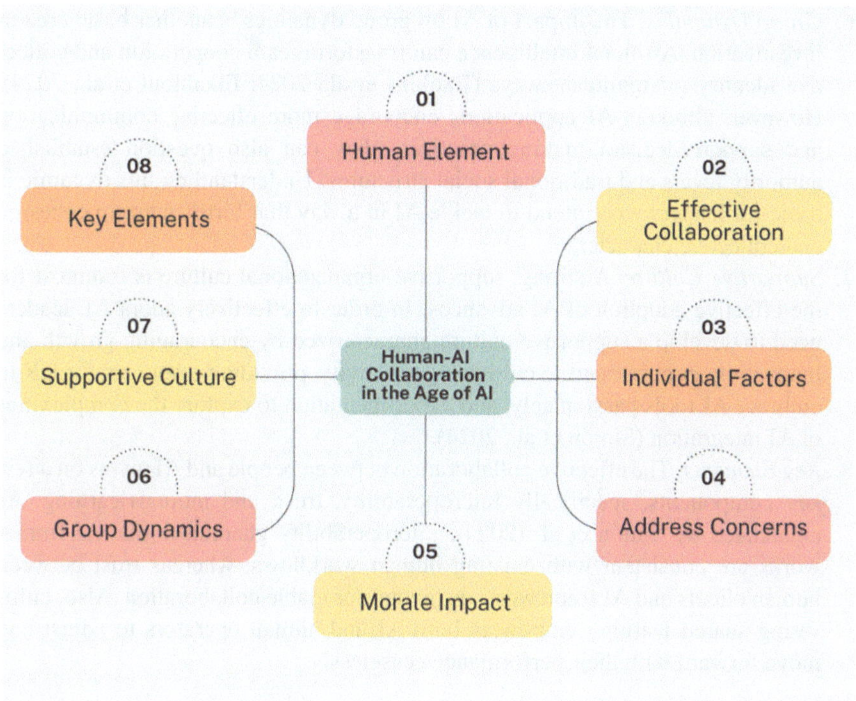

Fig. 2.1 Human–AI collaboration

point on AI are more likely to grasp innovative progressions, whereas work plans that join AI mindfully can upgrade engagement and execution. Moreover, the traits of AI, such as user-friendliness and reliability, play a basic role in forming HR experiences.

4. *Address Concerns*: The approach of AI within the work environment has produced legitimate concerns with respect to work security and the decline in the quality of skills. Gursoy and Cai (2025) emphasize the significance of tending to these tensions proactively. Organizations must execute techniques that console workers in almost all their roles in an AI-enhanced environment, maybe through reskilling programs and straightforward communication about the advancing nature of work. Organizations can relieve resistance and cultivate a more inviting atmosphere for AI integration by tending to these concerns.
5. *Morale Impact*: The presentation of AI innovations can altogether influence employee morale, requiring proactive measures to upgrade working environment fulfillment and engagement. Gursoy and Cai (2025) contend that organizations ought to prioritize activities to improve employee morale and make strides toward representative resolve amid periods of innovative change. These measures may incorporate open gatherings for discourse, recognition of employee commitments, and the establishment of support frameworks that empower collaboration between humans and AI partners.

6. *Group Dynamics*: The impact of AI on group dynamics is another basic area of investigation. Artificial intelligence can transform team cooperation and collective identity in significant ways (Bankins et al., 2024; Elkahlout et al., 2024). However, although AI applications encourage more effective communication and support decision-making practices, they can also question established authority levels and traditional social structures. Understanding this dynamic is basic for leaders who intend to tackle AI in a way that fortifies group cohesion and collective character.
7. *Supportive Culture*: A strong, supportive organizational culture is foremost for the effective adoption of AI advances. In order to effectively adopt AI, leaders need to develop a supportive culture characterized by encouraging growth and innovation, commitment to cultivating creativity, providing resources for HR to embrace AI tools passionately, and experimentation to explore the complexities of AI integration (Simón et al., 2024).
8. *Key Elements*: The effective collaboration between people and AI pivots on a few key components, specifically interoperability, trust, and mutual learning. As enunciated by Simón et al. (2024), interoperability guarantees that AI frameworks are consistent with existing human workflows, whereas trust between human clients and AI frameworks is pivotal for viable collaboration. Also, cultivating shared learning empowers both AI and human operators to adjust and move forward with their performance ceaselessly.

2.2.2 AI Adoption and Job Crafting: Reimagining Tasks and Roles

As AI is implemented in enterprises, the idea of "job crafting" becomes more and more essential. The proactive rethinking of work that strikes a balance between organizational demands, available resources, and human requirements is known as "job crafting." Job crafting, work design process, defined as proactive employee-initiated changes to task, relational and cognitive boundaries of their work (Wrzesniewski & Dutton, 2001), offers a valuable lens for understanding human adaptation in the context of artificial intelligence integration within human resources (Tims et al., 2013). By systematically enhancing demanding demands, decreasing limiting demands, and extending functional and social resources, workers can tailor their jobs. Utilizing the full potential of AI technology requires human–AI collaboration in addition to job building.

More creative and efficient problem-solving can result from collaborative models that combine human understanding with AI skills. For instance, three hybrid search processes, autonomous, sequential, and interactive, where human and AI collaboration yields a variety of answers to complicated issues, are identified by Raisch and Fomina (2023).

When AI increasingly automates existing HR work (e.g., hiring, payroll), job crafting theory argues that the employees themselves will deliberately reconfigure their roles. HR professionals may use job crafting knowledge strategically to inform an effective process of AI integration and to stimulate employees to expand their role boundaries in a manner that is beneficial for overall organizational effectiveness. The world of work and organization is set to transform again with the development and utilization of AI.

A new application of job crafting theory to AI technology is provided by Perez et al. (2022), who take into account how the learning algorithms affect the workers' work experiences from their point of view.

In response to AI, the workers reframed their employment cognitively and changed the bounds of tasks and relationships. Their job constructing behaviors can be broadly viewed as attempts to reposition their understanding of work, move toward more intimate relationships with clients, and rebalance their degrees of autonomy, which were first diminished by the arrival of AI. Figure 2.2 illustrates the three key Job crafting behaviors in response to AI in organizations.

In general, employees' job crafting also has ramifications for employees' supervisors, customers, and their work surroundings in terms of the meaning of the AI technologies and how they are employed. Employees' coordinated response across the three job crafting aspects highlights how crucial it is for these dimensions to function together in order to successfully change employees' work experiences and raise the human worth of their services (Perez et al., 2022).

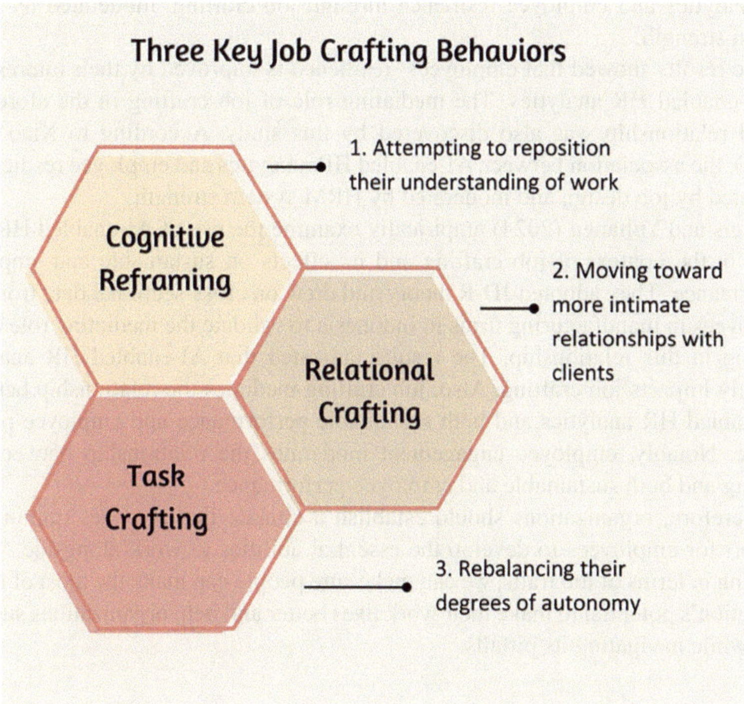

Fig. 2.2 Three key job crafting behaviors in response to AI (Perez et al., 2022)

Regarding Job Crafting of Employees in the context of (AI), the realization of AI under the backdrop of employees' work to restore has significant theoretical and practical significance. Employees must adjust to the work of artificial intelligence in the workplace, learn how to cooperate with artificial intelligence, and adjust to the relationship between processing and artificial intelligence.

As a result, they must redefine the meaning of the work when it is finished according to its working tasks and the change of the working relationship. They must also make cognitive and operational adjustments and fully utilize their own subjective initiative to complete a particular task.

Why Do Some Employees Craft Their Jobs to Adjust to AI, and Whether It Works?

Integrating the literature on AI and job crafting, Li et al. (2024) present the concept of AI crafting as a domain-specific type of job crafting and examine its results and antecedents. The results showed that leader AI crafting was positively related to employee AI crafting, which in turn was positively related to employee AI engagement and AI helping (Li et al., 2024). Hence, the research findings suggest a positive chain reaction (Fig. 2.3).

In order to highlight the contextual stimulus of AI-enabled HR analytics, Xiao et al. (2025) used two-wave surveys to gather data from 175 full-time hotel employees in China. Their goal is to investigate the indirect relationship between AI-enabled HR analytics and employee resilience through job crafting, moderated by HRM system strength.

The results showed that employees' resilience is improved by their impressions of AI-enabled HR analytics. The mediating role of job crafting in the aforementioned relationship was also discovered by this study. According to Xiao et al. (2025), the association between AI-enabled HR analytics and employee resilience is mediated by job design and moderated by HRM system strength.

Bagis and Yulianeu (2024) empirically examine the use of AI-enabled HR analytics in the context of job crafting and its effects on sustainable and employee performance. They adopted JD-R theory and drew on cross-sectional data from 349 employees in manufacturing firms in Indonesia to validate the mediating role of job crafting in this relationship. The results indicated that AI-enabled HR analytics strongly impacts job crafting. Also, job crafting mediates the relationship between AI-enabled HR analytics and both sustainable performance and employee performance. Notably, employee engagement moderates the relationship between job crafting and both sustainable and employee performance.

Therefore, organizations should establish a climate that provides training and support for employees to develop the essential abilities to work alongside AI. By thinking in terms of job traits, we can make sure people can make the most of the AI revolution's potential to make their work lives better and help organizations succeed even while navigating its pitfalls.

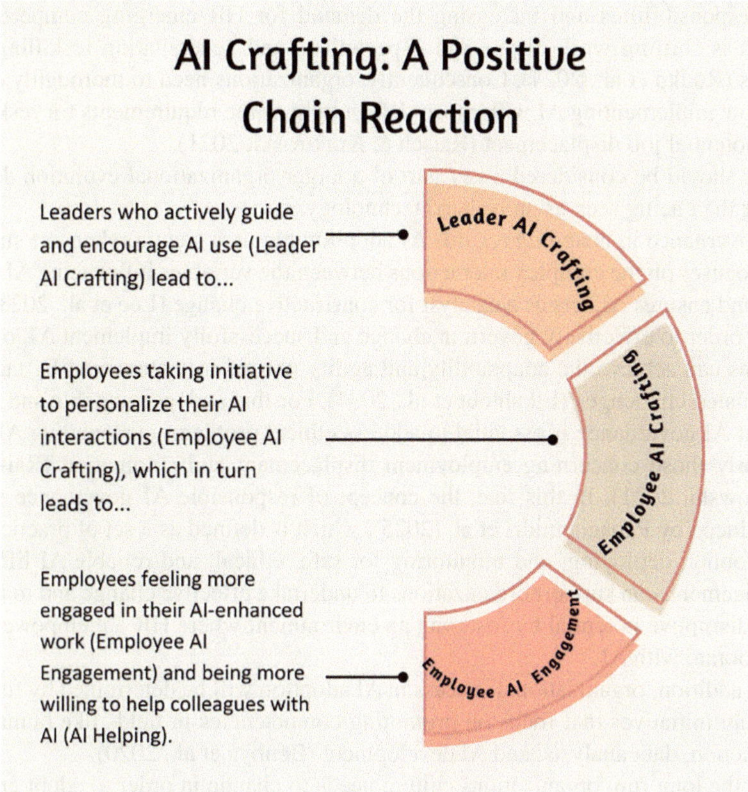

Fig. 2.3 AI crafting, a positive chain reaction (Li et al., 2024)

2.2.3 AI-Driven Workplace, HR Reskilling and Upskilling

In an AI-driven workplace, preparing HR and implementing reskilling and upskilling initiatives are crucial in response to the evolving requirements and changing demands of the workplace. As Mikalef et al. (2023) stated that human efforts to reskill and upskill are essential for adapting to emerging technologies in the digital era. AI technology supports productivity by automating tasks and simplifying procedures (Gendron et al., 2024), while it might result in job displacement. Therefore, reskilling programs and proactive HR planning are essential for negotiating this evolving landscape (Bankins et al., 2024). Due to the growing automation in the HR workplace, they need to learn new skills that complement AI applications (Mikalef et al., 2023). New skills such as soft skills, including critical thinking, creativity, and emotional intelligence are equally important as technical AI skills (Pillai & Sivathanu, 2020).

Organizational success will depend on funding training initiatives that emphasize enhancing competencies in fields including data analysis, AI development, and human–AI interaction (Benbya et al., 2020). Artificial intelligence is transforming job responsibilities and increasing the demand for HR emerging competencies, which is shifting work norms and expectations and necessitating reskilling programs (Rudko et al., 2024). Consequently, organizations need to thoroughly evaluate how implementing AI will impact HR in light of the requirements for reskilling and potential job displacement (Raisch & Krakowski, 2021).

AI should be considered a key part of a larger organizational evolution design, rather than being seen as an isolated technology.

Governance in changing regards AI adoption requires a comprehensive strategy that focuses on the complex interactions between the variables influencing AI adoption and ensures AI acts as a catalyst for constructive change (Lee et al., 2023).

In order to effectively govern in change and successfully implement AI, organizations can achieve the adaptability and agility needed to embrace AI by tackling the related challenges (Elkahlout et al., 2024). For this end, accountable and transparent AI governance is essential to address ethical problems surrounding AI, particularly those concerning employment displacement and automation (Raisch & Krakowski, 2021). In this line, the concept of responsible AI governance which introduced by Papagiannidis et al. (2025), which is defined as a set of practices for developing, deploying, and monitoring for safe, ethical, and reliable AI lifecycle management, can support organizations to undertake effective change and to utilize AI's disruptive potential by fostering an environment where HR are empowered to collaborate with AI.

In addition, organizational success in AI adoption will be determined by funding training initiatives that focus on promoting competencies in fields like human–AI interaction, data analysis, and AI development (Benbya et al., 2020).

In the long run, organizations culture needs to change in order to adopt an augmented workforce of AI. What leaders are going to need to create is a culture that rewards experimentation, continued learning, and ethical factors when deploying AI. Only organizations that can turn change to their advantage and unlock the revolutionary potential of AI technologies will thrive in these changing times by letting staff feel empowered to build and collaborate with AI.

2.3 Advantages and Benefits of Using AI in HR

The use of AI in HR brings several benefits that turn conventional HR processes into smart, strategic, and human-centric processes. The benefits fall under six broad categories:

2.3.1 Promoting Efficiency

Robotizing Repetitive Tasks: AI will be capable of automating all the mundane administrative work that comes under HR, including payroll processing, benefits, and new hire processing. According to Benbya et al. (2020), it also allows HR personnel to focus on strategic activities rather than administrative work.

Enhanced Strategic Planning: AI solutions enable a proactive rather than reactive HR approach by offering insights that match HR strategies with more general business objectives (Samir, 2024).

2.3.2 Improved Talent Acquisition and Management

Improved Recruitment: AI can help eliminate bias and improve hiring efficiency by automatically screening resumes and identifying the most qualified prospects (Pillai & Sivathanu, 2020).

Data-Enriched Talent Management: AI enables data to be managed to discover skill gaps and predict future needs of a talented employee pool, enabling strategic workforce planning (Mikalef et al., 2023).

AI-Enhanced Performance Management: AI tools facilitate ongoing feedback and analytics, leveraging personalized, tailored development plans and reducing review time spent on performance review processes (Ali Mohamad et al., 2023).

2.3.3 Personalized Employee Development and Experience

AI-Driven Personalized Learning and Development: AI customizes training to enhance skills and career development based on individual employee requirements, and customizes training programs to HR needs (Khushk et al., 2025).

AI-Augmented Worker Interaction: AIreinforces richer communication and interaction through virtual assistants and chatbots that provide instant responses to HR inquiries (Gursoy & Cai, 2025) are reinforced by artificial intelligence (AI).

AI-Future-Proofing Learning Programs: For HR competitiveness assurance purposes, AI facilitates future skills gap forecasting in occupations and guides HR toward efficient reskilling and upskilling (Rudko et al., 2024) (Fig. 2.4).

2.3.4 Promoting Agility and Cooperation

Promoting AI-Flexible Governance Strategies: AI implementation enables businesses to become more flexible in their governance strategies to allow them to respond promptly to market modifications (Rudko et al., 2024).

AI Decentralized Decision-Making: AI facilitates flatter organizational structure hierarchies to result in faster, local decision-making (Gladden et al., 2022).

Fostering Innovation: Increased problem-solving and novel solutions in the firm can be supported by an effective human–AI collaboration (Raisch & Fomina, 2023).

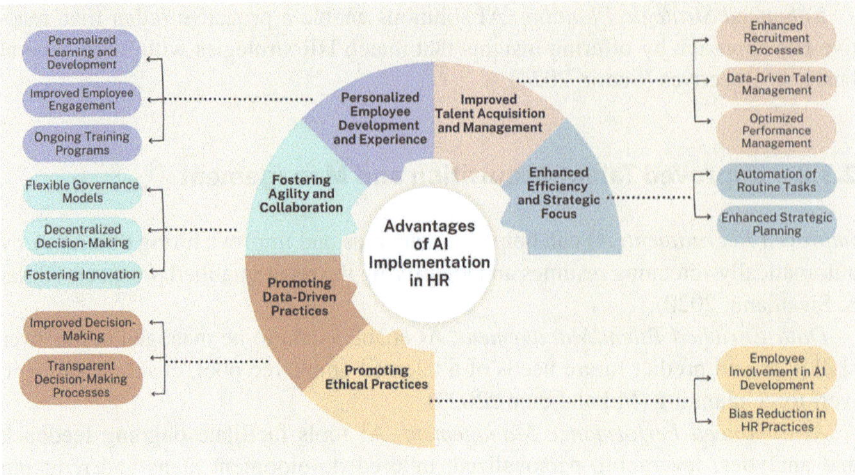

Fig. 2.4 Benefits of AI adoption in HR (Source: Systematic literature review)

2.3.5 Improved Data-Driven Decision

Faster and More Intelligent Decision-Making: AI allows immediate processing of data which helps HR departments make more informed decisions and respond to organizational requirements at a far quicker rate. This places HR processes in line with strategic objectives (Samir, 2024).

Accountable and Transparent HR Decisions: Organizations can have clear guidelines for the use of AI in HR for accountability as well as guaranteeing that ethical standards are followed (Papagiannidis et al., 2025).

2.3.6 AI Adoption and Foster Ethical Practices

Co-creation of AI by HR Engagement: Divya et al. (2024) propose that the involvement of employees in co-creating AI fosters acceptance and reduces resistance.

Reducing Bias in HR Decisions: AI attributes help identify and reduce biases in hiring and promotion decisions to increase diversity in the workplace (Robert et al., 2020).

2.4 Generative AI Integration in HR: Transformative View

Adoption of generative AI applications such as ChatGPT as an emerging technology in organizational settings adds transformational potential for application on many levels of business and management (Prasad Agrawal, 2024). Generative AI has revolutionized a number of organizational functions, and human resources (HR) is definitely one of them. Given the challenges of digital transformation for organizations, a realization of key drivers shaping the integration of GenAI into HR becomes crucial. Alzeiby et al. (2025) found that strategic intent and strategic HRM practices act as intervening mechanisms to direct the impact of AI implementation in HR on promoting employee engagement and experience.

By rationally making the right moves in each of these areas, businesses can unlock the power of Gen AI and the ability to generate a more dynamic, inclusive, and effective HR set of functions. Generative AI is a category of artificial intelligence capable of creating content, including text, images, audio, and video, in accordance with user input. This technology depends on highly complex machine learning methods, such as deep learning models that replicate how the thousands of neurons in the brain interact and learn to make decisions.

Generative AI works over three primary stages: training, tuning, and generation.

Training: The process by which the base model, often a large language model (LLM) used for text generation, is built/trained on large quantities of raw, unstructured data using deep learning algorithms.

Fine-Tuning: Train the base model for your specific task by feeding it labeled data applicable to the problem.

Generation: The model produces new content from the learned patterns and structures.

The results are continuously evaluated and refined by both developers and users to improve both the quality and relevance.

2.4.1 Generative AI Use Cases

Generative AI is unfolding as a revolutionary technology in the HR space with various applications that improve efficiency, strategic implementation, and general employee experience. The primary application of generative AI in HR, as shown in Fig. 2.5, is:

Automation: Generative AI automates repeatable HR tasks so that HR professionals spend less time on transactional work.

Analytics: Delivers sophisticated analytics that enable actionable insights around improved talent management and organization growth.

Intranet and Communication: Communication gets more effective with chatbots and content automation, improving the effectiveness of HR posts and keeping employees engaged.

Transforming Processes: Generative AI could change the face of talent acquisition, employee experience, and HR in the round.

Integration: Companies should start integrating generative AI tools to support their HR organizations.

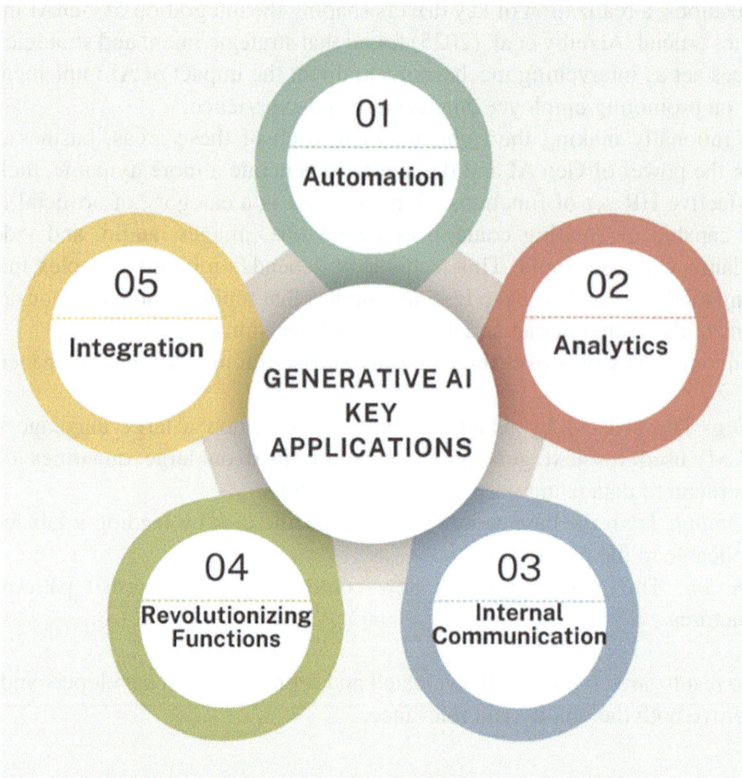

Fig. 2.5 Generative AI applications in HR

2.4.2 The Power of Generative AI for HR

The potential of generative AI, with its ability to process large data sets and generate human-like content, holds transformational promise for HR activities, including hiring, talent retention, employee engagement, and training. For example, GenAI has the potential to automatically pre-screen resumes, support personalized learning modules, and provide predictive analytics for workforce planning (Ooi et al., 2023). These abilities don't only make workflows more efficient, they also allow for more evidence-based decision-making and a more dynamic and flexible HR environment.

Holmström and Carroll (2024) note that the successful use of ChatGPT and the like necessitates strategic utility. Companies need to design innovation strategies to tap GenAI's strengths—whether that's enhancing creativity or streamlining operations while handling its inherent messiness. It is the necessity for a clear vision and structured implementation roadmaps that we must clear up to ensure that the technology potential is fully realized.

2.4.3 Relevance for Organizational Structure and Culture

The use of generative AI in HR can act as a trigger for an organizational reorganization. Baumann and Wu (2023) argue that automation, through AI, and collaboration support could break down hierarchical walls, establishing flatter twenty-first-century forms of organization or hybrids thereof. For HR, this might mean autonomous teams, distributed decision-making, and cross-functional working, all very much in tune with current thinking around agile working in organizations. However, these changes in structure have to be carefully managed. Change resistance, ethics, and possible job loss are challenges that need to be addressed actively with stakeholder involvement and open communication.

2.4.4 Ethical and Human-Centered Implications

As had been noted, although GenAI may generate entrepreneurial benefits, the deployment of GenAI must be based on ethical principles (Holmström & Carroll, 2024). The power of the technology to enhance or replace human creativity poses transparency, fairness, and job impact questions. For HR, which is rooted in trust and fairness, it is crucial to ensure that AI systems are ethically sound. For Design: Striking the balance between optimizing goals and preserving human dignity, privacy, and inclusivity.

2.5 Pitfalls of Rapid AI Adoption: Risks and Challenges

Adoption of AI may be hampered by mistrust of technology (Kolbjørnsrud et al., 2017), in contrast to conventional IT implementations.

It is certainly possible to initiate good change, but its implementation should be well understood in depth in relation to the challenges and dangers involved. A comprehension of the respective strengths and limitations of various AI systems is thus obligatory (Maragno et al. 2023). A general review reveals a complex network of interconnected dangers, such as

1. *Exacerbation of Current Inequalities*: One major worry is that AI may make preexisting societal prejudices worse.
2. *The Erosion of Human Skills and Critical Thinking*: Human critical thinking skills and deskilling are at risk as AI replaces humans in everyday activities and decision-making.
3. *Moral Conundrums in Self-Governing Systems*: Complex ethical conundrums are brought up by the development of autonomous technologies, such as self-driving automobiles.

In the event of an accident, who is responsible? How should the artificial intelligence system be configured to act morally when harm is inevitable? these issues need serious thought and the creation of precise ethical standards.

The monograph results show that AI implementation brings a dual set of issues: challenges, such as change resistance, data security concerns, and integration cost, are major inhibitors, but effective digital leadership, business culture, and developments in NLP and machine learning are key drivers (Madanchian & Taherdoost, 2025).

Governing in the AI Age

3

Abstract

This chapter discovers the new organizational governance world of the age of AI by focusing on the shift toward proactive instead of reactive leadership in a VUCA environment. It stresses the imperative of ethical AI governance through continuous practices in developing, deploying, and overseeing AI systems ethically, securely, and transparently throughout their life cycle. Centrally involved in this debate are two critical risks posed by biases, opaqueness, and ethics of AI, which require strong data governance frameworks, legal controls, and ethical standards to maintain social norms as well as organizational integrity. This chapter requires agile, adaptive models of governance that use AI in strategic decision-making, drive innovation, and allow organizations to move swiftly as a response to shifting external contexts. It emphasizes the contribution of AI toward reimagining organizational architecture, HR processes, and leadership skills, developing decentralized decision-making, reskilling, and responsible AI creation. It also talks about the intersection of AI and change management and recommends evidence-based frameworks and predictive analytics as drivers of long-term organizational shift. This chapter is wrapped up by the analysis of the dynamic regulatory environment, and more notably, international cooperation to balance innovation with ethical and privacy concerns to make proper adoption of AI work as per human values and societal expectations. In total, this in-depth analysis emphasizes that good governance in the age of AI demands a strategic, ethical, and responsive strategy for tapping the potential of AI and reducing its risks.

A. Rosa, *New Business Organizational Models for Governing in Times of Change*, Future of Business and Finance,
https://doi.org/10.1007/978-3-032-04091-6_3

The volatile, uncertain, complex, and ambiguous (VUCA) business environment of today poses previously unheard-of difficulties for organizations. With an emphasis on the pivotal shift from governing change to governing in change, this chapter examines this transformation. This calls for a reconsideration of conventional organizational models as well as the implementation of strategies that give attention to flexibility, agility, and above all ethical issues. This shift revolves around responsible AI governance (Papagiannidis et al., 2025).

Papagiannidis and Others: "A set of practices for developing, deploying, and monitoring AI applications in a safe, trustworthy, and ethical manner that ensures appropriate functionality of AI over the entire lifecycle" is how responsible AI governance is defined by (2025).

This definition emphasizes how responsible AI is a continuous and holistic process that is integrated into all phases of an AI system's lifecycle, from conception to eventual decommissioning. AI development and implementation alone are not enough. To make sure that their usage is consistent with moral expectations, social norms, and organizational goals, organizations need to establish robust monitoring protocols. This entails creating explicit data governance guidelines and guaranteeing data accessibility (Aldoseri et al., 2024; Lee et al., 2023). Effective deployment of AI is dependent on data security, quality, and availability; effective data governance models are necessary to support that data is available, secure, and reliable to be used with AI (Lee et al., 2023).

Artificial intelligence applications, especially those based on machine learning, tend to get biased, may have unforeseen effects, and, when not moderated adequately, even reinforce undesirable social trends. The "black box" problem, the very untransparency of AI decision-making built into it, is a challenge to knowledge and a roadblock to knowing how AI systems come to their conclusions. When not properly controlled, these factors can lead to unintended adverse impacts ranging from privacy breaches and bias to damage to one's reputation and erosion of public trust (Papagiannidis et al., 2025).

Therefore, it is a priority to develop ethical AI systems, and ethical and legal concerns come first at the top along with data quality and governance, and constructing explicit use cases (Lee et al., 2023).

Clear and transparent AI regulation is essential to allow companies to respond sooner and address the ethical issues of AI, especially job displacement and automation (Raisch & Krakowski, 2021). Strong ethical and legal structures addressing bias, accountability, transparency, and data privacy concerns are required in an effort to make sure AI is correctly developed and used (Gendron et al., 2024). Not only is ethical regulation of AI a moral imperative, but it is also strategic. Irresponsible AI governance risks damaging people and communities, as well as long-term company success, for those companies that are apathetic regarding responsible AI. Under the era of greater scrutiny and publicity, moral mistakes in AI can prove to have disastrous effects on reputation, customer loyalty, and even regulatory efficacy, as emphasized by Papagiannidis et al. (2025).

This is directly linked to the potential use of AI as a means of exerting excessive control. The governance of ethics is essential to prevent AI from being misused for extensive surveillance and control, maintaining that AI systems uphold worker autonomy and welfare (Bankins et al., 2024). AI is more than just a technical tool; it functions as an agent inside the company, influencing decisions, interacting with people, and making choices. Understanding AI's "entity" status is essential to comprehending how it affects organizational dynamics and the need for new leadership and governance models (Gladden et al., 2022).

Given that AI's automation potential changes job roles and generates a need for new skills, this has important ramifications for HR models and calls for reskilling initiatives (Bankins et al., 2024). Strategic alignment, sufficient financial, human, and technological resources, sufficient knowledge of AI literacy and skills, a collaborative and innovative culture, and high-quality data are all components of an organization's preparedness for AI (Jöhnk et al., 2021; Hradecky et al., 2022).

Success with AI is consistently attributed to quality, availability, and management. AI can also help create more agile processes, decentralized decision-making, and flatter organizational structures, which can challenge conventional management models and necessitate new organizational governance strategies (Rudko et al., 2024). Successful change governance is the competence to span the inner and outer worlds, enabling the organization to identify and act upon shifting marketplace requirements (Jarrahi et al., 2023). Managers can be worried about AI, particularly those in occupations with repetitive or rule-based work (Kolbjørnsrud et al., 2017). It is essential that these problems be solved using development and training. Some employees might be recalcitrant or less accepting of AI agent utilization because they are used to it (Lewandowski et al., 2021).

Clear employee benefit communication and upskilling are essential for an effective CA implementation. Organizations need to adopt a new governance paradigm that actively shapes change rather than merely responding to it in the dynamic and interconnected business environment of today. Olan et al. (2022) explain why knowledge sharing (KS) is vitally important in making it easier for organizations to transform, especially using AI. They argue that KS and AI complement each other but are also compatible, and each has the capacity to make the other better at innovation, enhancing organizational performance, and transcending challenges of the modern business environment (Olan et al., 2022).

Hence, firms need to implement a model of governance that is responsive, adaptive, and proactive in propelling transformation away from managing change and toward governing in it (Olan et al., 2022). Functions, responsibilities, and working procedures must be refashioned to utilize the capabilities of AI, and governance systems must be made compatible to integrate AI into existing working procedures. For the management of AI development, deployment, and upkeep, explicit governance systems (Lewandowski et al., 2021) are required.

This is consistent with how digital technology affects domains such as the government environment. Apart from process control optimization, profitability, competitiveness, customer satisfaction, and operational efficiency, AI can also change organizational business models, structure, and organizational culture (Lee et al., 2023).

3.1 AI and Agile Governance: Navigating Change

Agility and responsiveness are now necessary for an organization to survive and succeed in the fast-paced business world of today. Artificial intelligence (AI) makes responsive organizational governance possible to a very large extent. AI empowers human resources to be freed for strategic decision-making and adaptable response to market volatility through automating mundane tasks and providing real-time intelligence (Benbya et al., 2020). AI-based analytics promotes agile processes through providing data-driven feedback loops supporting ongoing learning and adjustment. A more flexible and responsive organizational structure that is better able to handle the intricacies of the contemporary business environment is produced by incorporating AI into agile frameworks.

The main idea of the monograph, that organizations need to learn to govern in change rather than just govern change, is directly supported by this. An essential part of managing change is dynamic adaptation. Organizations looking to prosper in a VUCA world now need to be able to move quickly (Taskan et al., 2022).

The capacity of AI to enable organizations to be responsive and timely to shifts in market conditions is supportive of agile values of customer obsession, collaboration, and flexibility. AI facilitation of decision-making improves organizational governance agility considerably.

Artificial intelligence (AI) computer systems analyze vast quantities of data in real-time, providing decision-makers with insights on which to base strategic adjustments. This is particularly significant in a rapidly changing environment, as conventional models of decision-making may fail (Shrestha et al., 2019). The incorporation of artificial intelligence (AI) into decision-making frameworks requires hybrid models that integrate AI capabilities with human judgment (Raisch & Krakowski, 2021).

Through analytics and predictive insights driven by AI, decision-making is being transformed from intuition to well-informed strategy (Elkahlout et al., 2024).

While AI automates routine decisions, enabling leaders to focus on intricate, strategic issues, the organization becomes more responsive and agile, enabling it to make well-informed decisions instantly (Elkahlout et al., 2024). The wide range of uses for AI technologies is what makes this transition possible (Benbya et al., 2020).

A transition to agile governance requires constant learning and adaptation. Human resources can be made available for more strategic uses by using AI for routine work. Furthermore, AI allows companies to track internal and external trends and thus make decisions ahead of time (Atanassova et al., 2025).

Nevertheless, in an attempt to avert pitfalls such as over-reliance on technology or forgetting human considerations, the application of AI should be sought with care (Mirsky et al., 2023). Based on Baumann and Wu (2023), there is a need for agile organizational designs because of the very fast pace of innovation in AI.

It is difficult to keep up with these innovations through traditional stiff hierarchies, so more fluid designs are needed in order to provide quicker decision-making and seamless integration of new technologies. Simpler organization forms, decentralized decision-making, and more flexible processes can be facilitated by AI, challenging the classical management models and requiring new organizational governance methods to be developed (Rudko et al., 2024).

For the transition from governing change to governing in change, this flexibility is essential (Olan et al. 2022).

Besides that, AI is transforming business and calling for new forms of leadership. As AI impacts strategy, capabilities, culture, and human–AI collaboration, leaders need to transform to become more visionary, agile, data-enabled, and people-centric leaders and acquire collaboration and ethical decision-making. It calls for commitment to apply AI ethically and continue learning. To implement AI, a culture of innovation is required, with space for mistakes and adaptive project management (Neumann et al., 2024). In today's evolving world, the older styles of decision-making have proven impractical, and AI provides an insightful perspective of data-driven agile decision-making (Shick et al., 2024).

3.2 AI-Powered HR: Managing Change Through Feedback-Informed Strategies

Organizations need to adopt the AI-fueled HR reinvention in a bid to spearhead change and, above all, shape the changing workplace. The human component is still essential. The role of HR must change to emphasize employee development, creating a culture of learning, and guaranteeing the moral and responsible application of AI. AI is essentially revolutionizing human resource management, not just the operational facets of businesses. AI-powered HR systems streamline procedures and free up HR professionals to concentrate on more strategic projects by automating tasks like performance management, onboarding, and recruitment (Benbya et al., 2020).

AI enhances talent management by carrying out skill gap analysis, predicting employee turnover, and customizing learning and development programs. AI can also aid in enhancing an inclusive and diverse work culture by minimizing bias used in recruitment and promotion decisions (Benbya et al., 2020; Robert et al., 2020). More nimble and responsive models centered on well-being and engagement of employees are substituting conventional HR models, which have a rigid structure and processes (Pillai & Sivathanu, 2020).

By shortening the time of recruitment, artificial intelligence is revolutionizing talent acquisition using automated resume screening and predictive analytics (Ali Mohamad et al., 2023).

By reducing the prejudices in selection, AI-powered tools optimize productivity and quality hire (Robert et al., 2020). AI would also facilitate job crafting, wherein employees are empowered to tailor their jobs to their strengths and interests, which will enhance retention and job satisfaction.

AI is revolutionizing performance management systems through data analytics for personalization of development programs, skill gap identification, and individualized feedback (Mikalef et al., 2023). Expectations and norms of work are being transformed into a new reality by AI, transforming how work operates and resulting in a demand for new skills.

Retraining programs are required, and this has significant ramifications for HR models (Rudko et al., 2024). Work roles and skills are being redefined by AI's automation potential, necessitating proactive organizational responses to the shifting skills landscape. As a result, HR must refocus its efforts from more conventional administrative duties to more strategic ones. AI frees up HR personnel to concentrate on strategic tasks like candidate relationship management and employer branding by automating numerous repetitive tasks (Pillai & Sivathanu, 2020). This increased effectiveness directly supports the organization's capacity to manage change by enabling HR to concentrate on higher-value tasks.

By enabling more agile procedures, decentralized decision-making, and flatter organizational structures, artificial intelligence (AI) is upending conventional management models and calling for new methods of organizational governance (Rudko et al., 2024). According to Pillai and Sivathanu (2020), HR must be prepared to adopt and use AI technologies, which calls for the infrastructure, expertise, and abilities needed to deploy and oversee AI-powered solutions. It is imperative to address any "stickiness" to conventional talent acquisition techniques and overcome resistance to change. AI benefits must be exhibited by organizations, and HR personnel must receive assistance and training.

AI has a wide range of effects on organizational transformation, especially in human resources. Automation enhances productivity via the release of HR personnel to manage strategic initiatives (Pillai & Sivathanu, 2020). Productivity, cost, and strategy are merely a few KPIs that are enhanced by the improved efficiency of AI in HR and, in turn, enhance recruitment, retention, and employee growth (Kulshrestha, 2024). AI enhances employee engagement through tailored content and immediate support (Ooi et al., 2023); it also enables more informed and data-driven HR decision-making and simplifies HR procedures by automating repetitive tasks (Ooi et al., 2023).

AI models may be biased, but with careful planning and oversight, human bias in HR procedures may be reduced, fostering equity and justice (Ooi et al., 2023). But implementing AI in HR presents serious ethical issues, especially with regard to justice and fairness (Robert et al., 2020).

A dedication to ethical AI is necessary for change governance, making sure that these technologies empower workers rather than take advantage of them. Robert et al. (2020) investigate how AI and organizational justice intersect in HR, offering a framework for creating moral AI systems that takes interactional justice into account and makes sure AI enhances human interaction rather than replaces it (Robert et al., 2020). Employee voice and value are essential. Organizational readiness must be carefully considered when implementing AI in HR (Smith et al., 2024).

It is essential to raise awareness and provide upskilling to close the readiness gap between employees and the organization. Data security and privacy, algorithmic bias, the possible absence of human interaction, the explainability and transparency of AI decisions, and more general ethical issues are some of the major obstacles (Ooi et al., 2023).

The future of work, employee perceptions, explainable AI, human–AI collaboration, bias-free AI models, ethical frameworks, and training for HR professionals in the AI-driven environment are just a few of the topics that need constant research and development to address these (Ooi et al., 2023).

3.3 Strategic Approaches to AI-Driven Organizational Change

3.3.1 Change Management in the Era of AI: Frameworks and Best Practices

The technology revolution is accelerating organizational change, especially with the implementation of "exponential technologies" like artificial intelligence (AI), the Internet of Things, and data analytics that are fundamentally reshaping the future of work. AI, for instance, has been at the center of economic and organizational discussions because of its far-reaching consequences in various sectors (Tambe et al., 2019).

Organizational transformation is the practice of changing people, events, and activities within a specific setting with the intention of improving organizational functionality and increasing effectiveness and efficiency. With this paradigm, change is now a top item on managerial agendas, with its implications being inherent from social, economic, as well as institutional viewpoints. The application of effective change management practices is very important for the enhancement of public service quality and efficiency.

Although all private-sector approaches are highly researched, their application in the public sector remains under investigation.

Piercy et al. (2013) evaluate the effectiveness of cross-functional team-based approaches through three case studies of local authorities. They identify four key elements for the success of cross-functional teams in the public sector. Three of these align with private sector findings: Clear Leadership Support: Strong backing from organizational leaders is crucial. Cultural and Structural Alignment:

A supportive culture and structure are necessary, though the public sector may require different applications than the private sector. Financial Resources: Sufficient funding is essential for team effectiveness. Additionally, Piercy et al. (2013) highlight a fourth factor: the need to challenge the status quo and address resistance to change. This insight emphasizes the unique challenges faced in public sector change initiatives.

Piercy et al. (2013) suggest that these conditions can be fulfilled within public organizations, advocating for the incorporation of cross-functional teams in public sector change efforts. By embracing these strategies, public organizations can enhance their change management processes and improve service delivery and effectiveness.

AI implementation into change management plans is a serious issue, especially brought about by the COVID-19 pandemic, causing new avenues in human resource management and change momentum. It helps in being instrumental in bringing long-term process change in companies.

The scholarly discourse on organizational change can be categorized into two predominant streams: one that emphasizes the identification of new resources and competencies to enhance an organization's capacity to create value and yield returns for stakeholders and a second that investigates innovative processes and models, including the role of AI in augmenting change management by enabling a more predictive and improvement-oriented approach (Berente et al., 2021). The organizational change management process is coming to be better understood as one of the key leadership competencies needed in today's times, given that organizations deal with dynamic external forces like globalization, technology, and changing labor demographics. Literature on this has two broad paradigms.

The first discusses the identification of new competencies and resources available to an organization to generate value and deliver returns to its stakeholders. The second stream entails placing the highest priority on reconciliation of management practice and scholarly knowledge to inform a successful change strategy.

The capacity of an organization to transform and leadership both facilitate to implement AI positively (Kurup & Gupta, 2022). AI transformation and change management both require an open environment questioning the status quo and embracing collaboration (Piercy et al., 2013; Zheng, 2024; Rožman et al., 2023). Figure 3.1 illustrates the link between organizational change capability, leadership, and AI adoption.

Stouten et al. (2018) argue that while many organizations struggle to implement meaningful and sustainable changes, there is a noticeable gap in the consensus within organizational research regarding fundamental change management processes and principles. This disjunction often results in practitioners relying on

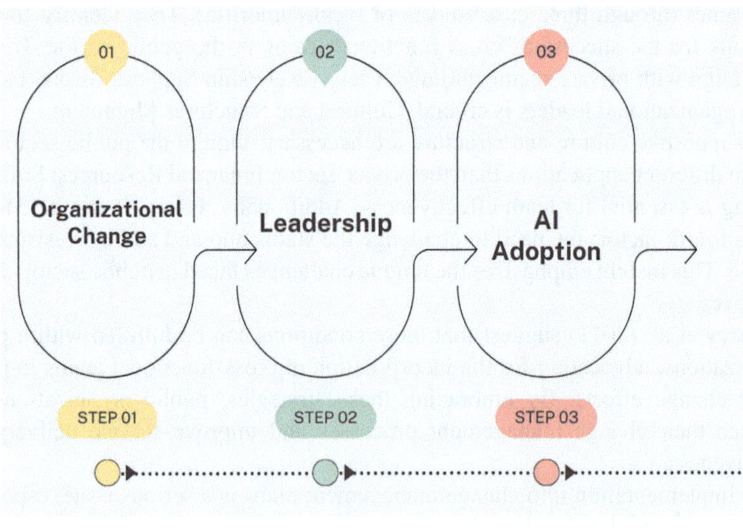

Fig. 3.1 The link between organizational change capability, leadership, and AI adoption

popular change models that lack robust scientific evidence, thereby undermining the potential for effective change initiatives.

Stouten et al. (2018) propose a synthesis of widely used prescriptive models of change management with empirical findings from scholarly literature. They identify ten evidence-based steps to conduct planned organizational change. The steps aim at narrowing the gap between theory and models and practice, hence improving chances for successful change as well as reducing the trauma of change to employees.

Major Steps for Organizational Change Management

1. *Evaluate the Problem or Opportunity Compelling the Change*: Collecting detailed information to diagnose the need for change. This process makes certain that the rationale for change is built on a solid understanding of organizational forces and stakeholder views.
2. *Select and Empower a Guiding Change Coalition*: Creating a coalition of leaders of change who can mentor the process of change is required. The partnership must be represented by several stakeholders and keep management in touch.
3. *Develop a Clear, Inspiring Vision of the Change*: An inspiring vision encourages individuals to seek out the change. It has to appeal to many stakeholders and be stated in terms that are inspiring but possible.
4. *Communicate the Vision*: Effective communication practices are necessary in an attempt to gain the vision accepted and implemented throughout the organization. This includes applying different forms of communication and maintaining communications open.
5. *Energize for Change*: Creating actual implementation plans, including readiness assessment and resource planning, will energize the organization to prepare for the change.
6. *Empower Others to Act*: Fostering employee initiative and participation is key to creating ownership and accountability in the culture throughout the change.
7. *Acquire and Foster Change-Related Knowledge and Competence*: The organizations have to spend money on training and learning to provide the employees with the skills and knowledge required to accommodate the changes.
8. *Identify Short-Term Wins*: The initial successes should be well recognized and celebrated to build up momentum and make the change effort appear well worth it.
9. *Monitor and Sustain the Change Process Over Time*: The system of feedback and evaluation should be implemented in tracking progress and adjusting accordingly.
10. *Institutionalize Change in Company Culture*: The changes should be embedded in the organizational culture, practices, and management succession process for them to be sustainable.

In summary, the integration of practice with academic evidence is an avenue for organizations to better manage the challenges of change. As work continues to unfold, embracing a more holistic and evidence-based style of change management will be key to sustaining success.

Lastly, the incorporation of management practice and academic evidence presents a way by which organizations will be able to handle change in a better way.

Among the most relevant for sustainable success was the increasingly integrative and evidence-based view of changing work. Prediction and analytics are central to organizational change management because they give leaders the power to make data-driven decisions, predict potential obstacles, and plan how to move through them. With corporations discovering mechanisms of adjustment to changing market realities, technologies, and internal transformations, predictive analytics enables companies to discover trends, predict results, and reducing risk.

Using machine learning algorithm applications, statistical modeling, and analysis of past data, organizations can forecast and anticipate employee reactions, project success rates, and possible implications of change efforts. An anticipatory mindset through decision-making enhances decision-making, decreases uncertainty, and supports a more responsive, agile culture. By applying predictive analytics to change management models, firms can better implement and deliver changes, enhance stakeholder participation, and maintain long-term success.

Organizational change management (OCM) is an imperative process that drives organizations into transformation processes to enhance efficiency, competitiveness, and flexibility. The explanatory and predictive roles played by artificial intelligence (AI) and predictive analytics toward business strategic intelligence, thus determining the nature of OCM. The authors investigate how advancements in machine learning and handling real-time data induce greater predictive accuracy and less delay in decision making.

Drawing on the theoretical models of the Technology Acceptance Model (TAM) and the Resource-Based View (RBV), the authors propose a conceptual model demonstrating how AI and predictive analytics have the potential to drive decision-making based on data. Such a factor plays a crucial role for companies that aim to optimize their competitiveness within the rapidly changing marketplace scenario.

Some of the crucial factors influencing the adoption of AI in an organization are data infrastructure capability, the degree of competency maturity of employees, and the ethics involved in using data. The paper stresses that it is important that AI system-based tools are implemented strictly focusing on data handling, establishing feedback loops at all times, and compliance with ethics. These are significant in such a way that not only do the organizations manage to integrate newer technology, but also have the capability to build a culture of responsiveness and innovation.

In short, through the support of AI and predictive analytics, organizations can improve decision-making, utilize resources optimally, and respond to market changes in time. Therefore, OCM must adopt such technological innovations as the major drivers of successful change in a way that assists organizations to adapt to the complexity of the modern business world. AI thus fosters novel change management models, enhancing the effectiveness of change strategies and facilitating predictive management in information systems projects while addressing organizational complexities (Tambe et al., 2019).

However, the adoption of AI is often hindered by insufficient organizational maturity and a lack of requisite change management competencies necessary for effective implementation (Shick et al., 2024). The swift evolution of organizations necessitates the establishment of strategic guidelines to adapt to the rapid changes instigated by AI (Trunk et al., 2020). Consequently, the convergence of change management and AI represents a burgeoning research frontier. Predictive change management powered by AI, as articulated by Trunk et al. (2020), could enhance organizations' capabilities to foresee change and surmount skill barriers, thereby fostering an ecosystem that amplifies the strengths of both domains.

In this context, Assochange, the Italian Observatory on Change Management, has designated the theme for 2024 as the development of organizations that effectively leverage the diverse generational capabilities in an increasingly technology-driven and AI-dominated environment. A recent Assochange survey of more than 100 organizations provided a change in thinking about change in 2017, 2020, and 2023. The proportion of organizations grasping change as a necessity and urgency for survival was 28% in 2017 compared to 31% in 2023, referring to increasing awareness regarding the role of change in a changing market. Also in 2023, 31% of organizations viewed change as top-of-mind only for certain strategic initiatives, like innovation and business model transformation, rather than a more binary approach in earlier years.

The belief in change as one of the key success factors, though with little effect on operational day-to-day management, reached 38% in 2020 and continued to be crucial at 31% in 2023. In this time, the number of organizations where change is not considered a priority declined to 1% in 2023, indicating a virtual global recognition of change as a strategic priority (Assochange, 2023). These results show a coming of age in change management, with firms increasingly seeing change as a strategic imperative but also as a means to innovate and respond to modern challenges.

Integration of AI into Change Management Processes

Artificial intelligence (AI) integration in change management (CM) processes has come to be a dominating theme of organizational research in our times. There are a number of authors who have penned works on the potential for change represented by AI and its use not only as an automation tool but as a means of total organizational change.

Role of AI in Organizational Change

Impact on Management Practices

Research by Popli and Rizvi (2016) emphasizes the radical enhancement of marketing and human resource management practices possible through AI implementation. This transformation is also in need of a fine strategy, and firms have to come up with clear guidelines to implement AI in everyday life. Cummings (2016) cites training and assisting employees throughout the whole process of change to achieve a seamless transition.

Resistance to Change and Leadership

Resistance to change has also been a pervasive theme in literature, and Tambe et al.'s (2019) research finds that cultural resistance of HR to change will be most likely to hinder the take-up of emerging technologies such as AI. In order to resist such resistance, organizations are recommended to pursue a transformational leadership style with the ability to stimulate acceptance and establish an innovation-permeable culture (Alamri, 2025). Good leadership should be able to counter employees' fears regarding new technologies, such as loss of control or a lack the skills.

Models and Frameworks for Effective Change

Literature offers a number of different models and frameworks through which the integration of AI into CM processes can be facilitated. Storbacka and Nenonen (2009) promote the creation of a theoretical framework to guide organizations through the stages of AI introduction and setting up, and spur strategic change. Lemos (2022) indicates the need for data-driven decision-making and organizations to instill a culture that can leverage AI.

Enhancing Organizational Performance Through AI

The majority of research highlights the capabilities of AI to boost firm performance. AI has the potential to revolutionize management practices and make them more productive and efficient. AI projects should be company-wide aligned in order to succeed in the long term.

Development of Skills and Capabilities

The general trend throughout the literature is one where organizations need to develop the capability and skills to properly apply AI (Tohãnean et al. 2020). Employee training needs to be continuous in order to defeat the fear of new technology and to inform employees of the opportunities of AI. Training should be supplemented with change management practices in order for AI adoption to be a success.

Briefly, the literature on the topic of the intersection of change management and artificial intelligence highlights that strategic alignment of AI into organizational processes is needed. This needs to be complemented by good leadership and commitment to continuous training as well as skills development. Resistance to change is a serious issue, but a scientific and well-informed approach can result in dramatic improvement in organizational performance and organizational culture change.

While learning has been accomplished, there remain broad gaps in the literature. For instance, empirical studies concerning the efficacy of AI in CM processes are few and far between, with most studies tending toward examining theoretical potential instead of concrete outcomes data (Popli & Rizvi, 2016; Cummings et al., 2016).

Theoretical structures for incorporating AI into CM models remain loosely developed.

In addition, theory and practice also remain apart from each other, where organizations cannot successfully implement AI technologies since there is no practical approach (Lemos et al., 2022). From a methodological perspective, stronger methods are necessary, like longitudinal research, to ascertain the long-term effects of AI.

Moreover, the research environment largely presents high-income nations, with little consideration of the specific issues encountered by firms in lower-income environments (Tohãnean et al., 2020). There is also no coherent and effective repository of detailed definitions and structures for terms such as "AI-driven CM" that may perhaps clarify the application of AI in change processes (Popli & Rizvi, 2016).

In total, there is immense potential for organizations to be able to build organizational ability, cultural renewal, and overall performance in change management if AI is applied in a purposeful and systematic way. More research is therefore required to plug the gap present by investigating how AI and CM interplay in various contexts so that organizational transformation can be effectively and sustainably implemented.

The following chapter will examine more deeply the business impacts of AI implementation in CM practices, illustrating how AI can deliver sophisticated tools for anticipating and managing change.

Regarding the conceptual overview of the figure (Fig. 3.2), it visually synthesizes the interconnected components of AI, agile governance, HR transformation, change management frameworks, and organizational capabilities. It clearly illustrates the flow from external drivers and context, including the VUCA environment, rapid AI innovation, data explosion, and market and workforce dynamics, to internal organizational responses, including organizational capabilities and foundations, leadership transformation, organizational culture, structural flexibility, and change readiness and competencies. In the framework, AI-enabled strategic pillars include AI and predictive analytics, AI in governance and decision-making, AI in HR management, and AI in change management.

Fig. 3.2 Effective organizational change governance and integrating AI-driven strategies (Source: Systematic literature review)

3.4 Designing Moral AI Systems

While the deepening roots of artificial intelligence (AI) in business processes bring unprecedented opportunities never dreamed of, it also brings some serious ethical concerns. Creating ethical AI systems is not a virtuous cause alone; it is an imperative for survival of companies that wish to be able to manage change.

AI is influencing workplace ethics and values as it becomes more integrated into operations (Agrawal, 2024). It is imperative to give ethical AI development top priority in order to guarantee that AI systems are created and applied in a way that prioritizes human values (Olan et al., 2022).

According to Papagiannidis (2025), responsible AI governance is "a collection of procedures for creating, implementing, and overseeing AI applications in a secure, reliable, and moral way that guarantees proper operation of AI throughout its whole lifecycle."

Developing and implementing AI alone is not enough. Addressing potential social dysfunctions brought on by the use of AI, such as algorithmic bias, inexplicable decision outcomes, a blurring of accountability boundaries, and invasions of privacy, is part of this (Benbya et al., 2020). The case for moral AI systems revolves around these issues, which need to be addressed head-on. For organizations looking to use AI to govern change, ethical considerations are crucial. Creating rules and regulations for the ethical and responsible application of AI is part of this (Agrawal, 2024).

Both essential steps (ethical frameworks, training, audits, stakeholder involvement, certifications, and diverse teams) and supplementary elements (regulation, human-centered design, transparency, open innovation, and sustainability) are included in a multifaceted framework for the ethical application of AI. Four ethical AI pillars are outlined in the chapter: aligning strategic drivers, facilitating human development, building trust and transparency, and values integration. Not only is ethical AI ethically sound but is also critical to building credibility and ensuring long-term success. Firms must address ethical concerns head-on by developing policies and legislation for the ethical and moral use of AI (Agrawal, 2024).

This supports the main contention of the book, which is that proactive ethical considerations must be addressed in order to govern effectively in times of change and guarantee that AI systems are implemented sensibly and in accordance with human values.

Understanding end users' viewpoints on AI adoption, including biases and ethical considerations, requires user-centric research (Misra et al., 2023). This involves comprehending how individuals view the relative advantages and disadvantages of algorithmic and human capabilities (Bankins et al., 2024). The need for moral AI systems that are regarded as just and reliable is further supported by workers' opinions on objectivity, decision-making procedures, and possible bias, all of which have an impact on their acceptance of AI.

Successful AI integration necessitates a comprehensive strategy taking into account ethical considerations, employee perceptions, and customer trust, as Gursoy and Cai (2025) show. Collaboration between humans and AI, ethical AI systems, and reskilling all rely on a positive corporate culture.

Leaders need to foster cultures that value creativity, human growth, and moral AI practices. The necessity of taking cultural dynamics into account for effective change governance is reinforced by case studies that show how culture affects the success of AI integration. Though it has several benefits, its implementation can become challenging. Change resentment, ethical issues, and threats to data security have to be addressed. If employees are engaged during change process, training is provided, and effective communication is upheld, organizations can effectively handle change. For successful development and utilization of AI ethically, ethical frameworks and control procedures have to be set up. For personal data protection and for building confidence, robust cybersecurity needs to be enforced (Elkahlout et al., 2024; Rudko et al., 2024). Responsible and moral use of AI systems is ensured by mechanisms for regulation and control (Holmström & Carroll, 2024).

Creating a cooperative atmosphere where AI and people can collaborate well is also crucial (Holmström & Carroll, 2024). According to Holmström and Carroll (2024), it is critical to address any potential ethical issues pertaining to bias, privacy, and job displacement. Developing human–AI collaboration techniques, concerning the ethics of AI governance, creating an ecosystem in which humans and machines can operate well together, and constructing systems to facilitate human–AI collaboration are all encompassed (Gladden et al., 2022). To meet moral and ethical challenges, fill the knowledge gap between humans and AI, translate AI-driven knowledge to strategic decision-making, and promote human–AI partnership, managers are essential (Baumann & Wu, 2023).

This calls for a reassessment of conventional leadership roles and duties. Leaders must enhance their capability to read insights generated by AI, understand its limitations, and make sound decisions by weighing AI suggestions against human and ethical values (Shick et al., 2024). This entails mitigating bias in training data, blackbox AI models, and ethical problems with AI decision-making (Shick et al., 2024).

Ethical AI systems that are open, responsible, and consistent with human values must be given top priority by organizations. It requires a trusting culture, teamwork, and continuous learning to effectively deploy AI (Shick et al., 2024; Jarrahi et al., 2023).

Maragno and associates (2023) examine the ways in which various factors produce both affordances and constraints for the application of AI.

Transparency, algorithmic bias, and data privacy are among the most significant ethical issues (Lee et al., 2023). The companies have to undertake positive measures to address such issues and make sure that the AI platforms meet the legal and ethical requirements. By remaining in contact with human needs, organizational values, and ethical standards, knowledge sharing (KS) may be utilized to inform the deployment and development of AI (Olan et al., 2022).

For conversational agents (CAs), ethically significant issues such as algorithmic bias, data privacy, and transparency of systems are applicable (Lewandowski et al., 2021). Organizations should make CAs develop and deploy ethically and responsibly, upholding user privacy and fairness. Both a business and moral imperative exist in the development of ethical AI systems. The ethical ramifications of increasingly integrated AI systems become critical.

Building ethical AI systems that are transparent, unbiased, and accountable should be the highest priority of an organization. The data should be free from bias and representative, requiring precise attention. Accountability and trust rely on the decision-making processes of AI systems being transparent.

Firms should have clearly established policies and guidelines on creating and implementing AI with infusion of moral considerations at all stages (Benbya et al., 2020). Prioritizing human values and social norms, ethical regulation of AI necessitates the development of systems that guarantee AI systems are being responsibly developed and deployed (De Cremer & Narayanan, 2023).

Algorithmic bias, data privacy, and accountability of AI decision-making are just some of the challenges which organizations must address proactively. Setting up moral guidelines, periodic auditing of AI systems, and creating an open culture are some of the numerous pieces of this multifaceted plan (Curtis et al., 2023).

The figure (Fig. 3.3) is a graphical representation of the multidimensional strategy of creating responsible AI systems with strategic alignment, stakeholder engagement, trust establishment, and organizational culture.

The four principal pillars of responsible AI systems, each an area of high-priority focus, are

Pillar 1: Strategic alignment and values: Align AI efforts with human-centric values and organizational values. Incorporate ethical values and ethical rules of governance.

Pillar 2: Transparency, regulation, and trust in algorithmic decision-making: There is regulation and standard-setting, and governance is defined.

Pillar 3: Human-focused model and integration of stakeholders: Employee engagement and end-user contribution in participatory design reduce biases, perceptions, and ethical issues.

Pillar 4: Change and culture involves developing a culture focused on development, ethics, and innovation within the organization, often implemented through training, communication, and upskilling programs. The responsible AI adoption-enabling strategies are ethical principles and guidelines; stakeholder engagement and user feedback; regulation and certification; and continuous audits and monitoring.

3.5 Regulatory Discussions of AI Adoption

Present discussions of AI regulation involve building comprehensive frameworks of data protection, transparency of algorithms, and regulatory norms at the national and international levels. The initiatives try to manage privacy, security, and responsibility issues while AI penetrates all sectors of businesses.

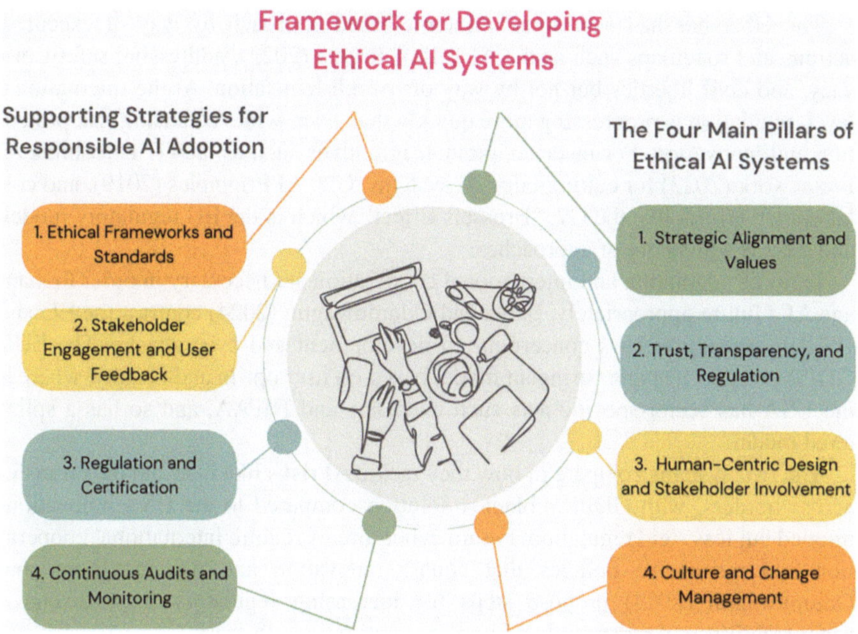

Fig. 3.3 Responsible, ethical AI systems, and suitable supporting strategies (Source: Systematic literature review)

Zharova (2023) mentions the inclusion of information security into legislation for protection against data breaches according to the EU's "privacy by design" approach. Transparency is also featured, where organizations are called on to reveal algorithm operations in order to foster trust and accountability. Both the EU and nations such as Russia are coming up with regulations to ensure responsible AI development.

Overall, such regulations serve to balance innovation and safeguard basic rights via legal proceedings that guarantee safe and ethical AI systems.

The Cole (2024) report gives a snapshot of how AI regulation and governance are across the world. It is observed that, in the wake of AI's transformative effect, policymakers globally are moving away from ethics principles to actual legal structures.

Some of the key international initiatives are the OECD AI Principles (2019), calling for responsible AI based on core values like human rights, transparency, and accountability; UNESCO's Recommendation (2021), with emphasis on ethics values and environmental protection; and the Council of Europe's work toward the establishment of a legally binding framework convention on the premises of human rights and democracy.

Regional endeavors are interwoven with the European Union's proposed AI Act (endorsed in 2024), proposed to establish an all-encompassing, risk-based framework of regulation exportable to member states with extraterritorial application for AI systems operating on the territory of the EU.

The USA has had a sectoral, principle-based approach by way of executive actions and roadmaps such as the AI Bill of Rights (2022), addressing safety, privacy, and civil liberties but not by way of overall legislation. At the international level, regulation is progressing more quickly than ever, while balancing risk protection and innovation. For instance, premier initiatives such as the G7 Hiroshima AI Framework (2023) for cutting-edge AI systems, G20 AI Principles (2019), and collaborative efforts like the G7, "Brussels Effect" which is the EU regulatory model, and the US's diversity of approaches.

Periodic adaptation and international cooperation are necessary in order to manage AI's future appropriately. Ijaiya and Odumuwagun (2024) contrast the EU and US data protection laws concerning AI development and cyberattacks. The EU's GDPR presents a single, stringent model based on user opt-in and penalty, whereas the USA has sector-specific acts such as CCPA and HIPAA, and so has a splintered model.

The two systems compare in how they tackle AI risks like bias and data transfer across borders, with GDPR's blanket solution compared to the US's innovation-minded but less rigid regulation. Future cyber threats require international cooperation and responsive policies that equate innovation and privacy. Ijaiya and Odumuwagun (2024) propose steps for increasing regulatory responsiveness, accountability, and responsible AI implementation in both areas.

Leadership in the AI Age

4

Abstract

This chapter provides a preview of the key role being played by senior management commitment to propelling AI take-up, aligning organizational capability, strategy, and culture and overcoming ethical, technical, and organizational barriers. It calls for developing new leadership competencies—data literacy, critical thinking, and ethical stewardship—so that one can lead AI-driven transformation and generate ethically responsible innovation. This chapter also proposes the necessity of robust human–AI collaboration in the form of co-workflows, experience-based learning, and responsible AI stewardship. This chapter applies models like TOE and diffusion of innovation to explore drivers and barriers of AI adoption and conquering resistance and technology issues.

The application of AI is more than a technological advancement; it is a paradigm shift in the way businesses work and compete. The role of leadership in leading through this transition is examined in this chapter, including the impact of AI deployment on leadership and the most important skills required to lead through change and not manage it.

In the context of implementing AI, an authentic-transformational leadership approach is essential. Leadership for the age of AI is a new set of abilities. Leaders must be cognizant of the AI possibility and capable of working through the complex organizational and ethical challenges it presents. Sponsorship by top management is necessary to make resource allocations, alter culture, and drive AI initiatives (Agrawal, 2024). AI is changing business and necessitates a new leadership style (Agrawal, 2024). The effect of AI on strategy, capabilities, culture, and human–AI relations calls for responsiveness from leaders. For purposes of instilling

A. Rosa, *New Business Organizational Models for Governing in Times of Change*, Future of Business and Finance,
https://doi.org/10.1007/978-3-032-04091-6_4

cooperation and moral judgment, they must be data-literate, human-focused, vision-driven, and agile (Agrawal, 2024). In order to effectively govern change, ongoing learning and a dedication to responsible AI implementation are called for.

It is likely that companies with a culture of innovation and are eager to try new things will utilize generative AI (Agrawal, 2024). The leadership plays a key role in providing the enabling environment. Organizational policy must center on risk-benefit analysis, strategic alignment, leadership support, cross-functional collaboration, and continuous improvement (Lee et al., 2023).

Kurup and Gupta (2022) are of the opinion that organizational ability to change and leadership influence AI implementation in a positive way. This transition to AI-driven decision-making has to redefine the traditional leadership function and role. Leaders have to develop new skills in, among other things, interpreting AI indications, comprehending the limitations of AI systems, and making informed decisions balancing AI advice against ethical and humanitarian considerations. Making decisions is no longer the main focus; instead, AI-driven decision-making systems that support organizational objectives and values are designed and put into place. This calls for a new set of leadership abilities, such as critical thinking, data literacy, and the capacity to encourage human–machine cooperation (Shick et al., 2024). Building organizational AI capabilities is essential, in addition to individual leadership competencies.

According to Gladden et al. (2022), AI actively participates in supervision, decision-making, and even leadership, necessitating the development of new governance and leadership models. An empowering culture and aligned leadership are necessary for capability renewal through vigilant learning, which empowers staff members to act as learning agents (Atanassova et al., 2025). According to Olsson et al. (2025), managers in the context of Industry 5.0 should respond to the demand for a more human-centric viewpoint by emphasizing organizational prerequisites like inclusive organizational change, leadership practices, learning and innovation processes, and holistic understanding.

4.1 Driving AI Adoption

For Industry 4.0, AI in HR is essential (Smith et al., 2024). AI must be incorporated into HR procedures if businesses are to prosper in the current technological environment. A quantitative evaluation of the effects of AI-driven HR practices on key performance indicators (KPIs) such as cost-effectiveness, strategic alignment, and employee productivity is the goal of the research (Smith et al., 2024). AI appears to simplify and enhance HR decision-making, especially when it comes to talent-related decisions, according to preliminary findings (Smith et al., 2024). Understanding the impact of AI adoption requires this data-driven understanding, which was acquired through surveys, data analysis, and case studies (Smith et al., 2024). To guarantee that AI initiatives support overarching organizational goals, this strategic alignment is necessary.

Benbya et al. (2020) observe how even though artificial intelligence is "now considered the most significant and revolutionary new technology for big organizations," there are a large number of individuals who are only just beginning to adopt it. Gursoy and Cai (2025) mark the extent to which revolutionary AI is by pointing out its myriad applications, ranging from chatbots and service robots to predictive models and targeted advertisements. They emphasize that an effective strategy with ethics in mind, employees' perception, and trust of the customers must be achieved for integration.

Organizational culture and AI adoption are closely related; hence, adoption of AI requires innovative and encouraging cultures (Rudko et al., 2024). The adoption of generative AI in organizations is the main topic of this chapter since it is essential to successfully managing change. It contends that although generative AI has enormous potential, a thorough grasp of the variables affecting its adoption and application is necessary to fully realize its transformative potential (Agrawal, 2024). Generative AI is more likely to be adopted by companies with an innovative culture and a willingness to try new things. Additionally, in order to promote AI adoption and create a positive atmosphere, leadership is essential (Agrawal, 2024). In order to promote AI adoption and allocate the required funds, leadership is essential (Agrawal, 2024).

A useful lens for analyzing these elements is the technology–organization–environment (TOE) framework, which is enhanced by institutional theory and diffusion of innovation theory (Agrawal, 2024). Coercive and mimetic institutional pressures can have a big impact on AI adoption because companies may use generative AI to stay ahead of the curve or meet industry standards. The diffusion of innovation theory identifies a number of variables that affect adoption rates, including perceived relative advantage, compatibility, trialability, complexity, and observability.

Top management support, organizational culture, competitive pressure, and institutional norms are important factors that influence the adoption of generative AI (Agrawal, 2024).

Despite the great potential of AI to enhance decision-making effectiveness and quality, managerial resistance often prevents it from being implemented on a large scale (Brink et al., 2024). Brink et al. (2024) identify the internal individual characteristics, demographics, familiarity, psychology, and personality affecting the attitudes of managers toward AI decision-making. Knowledge of these individual factors is necessary to design particular strategies for AI adoption. Establishing expertise, integrating AI into core business processes, and improving AI capabilities all require time and money from organizations (Ştefan et al., 2024). The positive feedback loop between organizational agility, AI use, and digital capabilities gets stronger as organizations get more experienced with AI adoption, resulting in a positive feedback loop that promotes continuous improvement (Ştefan et al., 2024).

Industry trends, competitive pressures, and technological infrastructure all have a big impact on the adoption of AI (Maragno et al., 2023). This chapter explores these crucial areas, referencing previous studies (Lee et al., 2023) to offer a thorough comprehension of the technological, organizational, informational, and human aspects of AI adoption. It covers informational issues such as data management, ethical and legal issues, and AI–human cooperation.

It also examines human and technological challenges, such as staffing issues, customer acceptance, and lack of expertise, as well as AI limitations and system integration (Lee et al., 2023). Olan and associates (2022) stress the importance of information exchange in helping organizations manage change, especially when it comes to the adoption of AI. Kolbjørnsrud et al. (2017) point out that adopting AI successfully calls for more than just purchasing new equipment.

Lewandowski and associates examine the elements affecting the integration and uptake of conversational agents (CAs) powered by AI in 2021. The main drivers of AI adoption in talent acquisition and their effects on organizational transformation are examined by Pillai and Sivathanu (2020). AI readiness is also influenced by organizational size, culture, and structure (Neumann et al., 2024). Government rules, industry demands, and competitive pressure are examples of external environmental factors that also come into play. Customer readiness is essential, especially in industries where there is a lot of interaction with customers (Neumann et al., 2024).

Cao et al. (2021) explore the elements that affect managers' decision-making acceptance or reluctance to use AI. Gendron et al. (2024) explain the paradoxical promise of AI, acknowledging its revolutionary potential and also its own risks and limitations. Sandkuhl (2019) urges an integrated approach to AI implementation that prioritizes the organizational context. Kurup and Gupta (2022) use the diffusion of innovation and technology–organization–environment theories to create a model that identifies the factors influencing the adoption of AI. Chiu et al. (2021) examine how the success of AI implementation is impacted by employees' pre-adoption attitudes toward the technology. Misra et al. (2023), Mahboub and Ghanem (2024), and Esmaeilzadeh (2024) emphasize the necessity of user-centric research that takes into account the biases and ethical ramifications of AI systems. Hradecky and colleagues examine the variables affecting AI adoption in the exhibition industry in 2022. Transformational leadership that sets up a culture of experimentation and learning, a strong vision, and a sense of urgency is required for AI to be adopted. Moreover, leaders should directly address the employees' worries and provide the training and assistance required for adaptation (Benbya et al., 2020).

In order to implement AI effectively, they need to overcome various kinds of barriers, e.g. organizational barriers, technical barriers, and environmental barriers (Misra et al., 2023). It is critical to recognize the significance of a systematic evaluation process in addition to the already thorough discussion of the factors influencing AI adoption. Businesses must evaluate their preparedness for implementing AI, which entails comprehending the organizational, technological, and environmental elements that either support or impede integration (Neumann et al., 2024). Leaders can assess these dimensions with the help of the technology–organization–environment (TOE) framework.

In particular, it is important to stress the following points:

Technological Dimensions: As a move to identify whether the existing IT infrastructure can accommodate integrating AI systems, caution is required when assessing. While creating a solid base for AI capabilities, organizations may be prompted to spend money on modernizing their technology (Sandkuhl, 2019). This covers accessibility and data infrastructure in addition to hardware and software.

Organizational Factors: Encouraging innovation and flexibility lies at the core of AI adoption. For enabling minimization of resistance and making integration of AI acceptable, there should be aggressive insistence on open communication and collaboration by executives (Shrestha et al., 2019). The cornerstones of such a change in culture are battling the fear of job loss among employees and permitting opportunities for reskilling and upskilling.

Environmental Factors: Organizations can manage external pressures to adopt AI by having astute awareness of the competitive climate and regulatory expectations (Maragno et al., 2023). Closing the knowledge gaps and building confidence in working with AI tools are two of them (Cao et al., 2021).

Training curricula that are specifically designed to meet the requirements and concerns of various employee groups are crucial.

Organizational Goals and AI Alignment: AI projects ought to be closely matched with the strategic goals of the company. Leaders must clearly define their vision for integrating AI, showing how it advances more general organizational objectives and produces measurable business results (Pillai & Sivathanu, 2020).

Promoting an Experimentation Culture: Teams can investigate AI applications and gain knowledge from mistakes by promoting an experimental mindset. This is founded on innovation and continuous improvement (Gendron et al., 2024).

4.2 Building Human–AI Collaboration: The Future of Partnerships

Likewise, the collaborative operation of humans with AI systems is equally as crucial to the possibility of transformation in AI as technical perfection. The development of this important collaboration is examined in this section, with a focus on a comprehensive strategy that takes organizational, group, and individual dynamics into account. As Bankins et al. (2024) stress that successful human–AI collaboration is necessary to achieve the full benefits of AI, necessitating a thorough comprehension of these complex influences.

Building organizational AI capabilities is crucial. These capabilities include having access to knowledgeable IT specialists, having a comprehensive understanding of AI technology throughout the company, being flexible, having high-quality data, receiving AI training, and creating internal AI solutions.

These are the cornerstones of an effective human–AI partnership. Leaders will also need to cultivate the strengths of humans and machines to work together and create mutual respect and trust to form such a partnership (Benbya et al., 2020).

Also, creating a positive, AI-ready culture and fostering effective collaboration. In addition, the managers need to take into consideration the following significant cases:

Develop a Clear Vision of and a Strategic Roadmap for AI Adoption: Companies need to articulate a clear vision for AI adoption and a strategic roadmap for implementation.

Promote a Culture of Change Management: Organizations should create a culture that embraces change and tries new things.

Break Down Organizational Silos and Foster Collaboration: AI can facilitate collaboration between teams and departments. In fact, employees should be given the chance to collaborate on AI-related projects and exchange knowledge and skills. The importance of employee perceptions in a successful AI integration is clarified by Gursoy and Cai (2025). Although AI has several benefits, they note that workers might feel apprehensive about job security, rendered obsolete by skills, and a changing workplace scenario. Personalized reskilling schemes, transparency, and prioritizing the development of human–AI partnerships are essential means of overcoming them. Bankins et al. (2024) mention the following five major themes that pertain to AI in the workplace: worker attitudes, perceptions of capabilities, human–AI collaboration, AI as a control mechanism, and labor market implications.

These themes reinforce the need for a comprehensive approach to "governing in change" by providing a thorough understanding of the complex effects of AI. In order to foster this collaboration, leaders should encourage knowledge of AI capabilities; leaders should make sure that staff members are aware of the advantages and disadvantages of AI technologies. Training on the proper use of AI tools to improve productivity and decision-making is part of this (Shick et al., 2024).

Creating Collaborative Work Processes: Businesses must create processes that combine AI and human capabilities. To foster cooperation and make AI augment human capabilities, duties and roles need to be redesigned (Holmström & Carroll, 2024).

Facilitating Iteration and Feedback: There should be channels of ongoing feedback among workers and AI systems by managers. AI tools can be continuously improved and aligned with organizational needs thanks to this iterative process (Azzam & Beckmann, 2022).

AI is revolutionizing business and requiring new kinds of leadership. This calls for ongoing education and a dedication to using AI responsibly. Increased automation and autonomy, improved human–AI collaboration, and the growth of AI-driven personalization are characteristics of the future of AI in organizations (Elkahlout et al., 2024). This future will be significantly shaped by ethical and regulatory developments. According to Baumann and Wu (2023), generative AI may lessen the need for conventional hierarchies if it can actually facilitate collaboration. Flatter structures or hybrid models may result from this. Ooi and associates (2023) look into the best ways to combine AI and humans in HR procedures to increase productivity while maintaining a human touch.

The character of work is changing with an emphasis on human–AI collaboration and the need for new skills. Thus, it becomes a formula for success for companies that want to thrive in the era of AI by leveraging this collaboration to the maximum extent. Lastly, it rests with leaders to create understanding, develop collaborative workflows, and overcome any obstacles to make human–AI collaboration succeed. Organizations would only be able to leverage the complete potential of AI integration if they implement it as a collaborator and not a replacement.

4.3 Ethical AI Governance: Leading with Integrity in the Age of AI

This book makes the case that managing the AI-driven transition requires a fundamental rethinking of conventional organizational models and the adoption of new strategies that place an emphasis on flexibility, agility, and, most importantly, ethical considerations. The idea of responsible AI governance is essential to this change.

Papagiannidis et al. (2025) propose a set of procedures for creating, implementing, and overseeing AI applications in a secure, reliable, and moral way that guarantees proper AI operation throughout its whole lifecycle is known as responsible AI governance. Responsible AI must be integrated into every phase of an AI system's development, from initial conception to continuous operation and eventual decommissioning, as this definition emphasizes. It is not enough for organizations to just create and implement AI; they also need to set up strong oversight procedures to make sure that their application is in line with moral standards, societal norms, and corporate objectives.

Bankins et al. (2024) explore how AI is used in algorithmic management, emphasizing AI as a control mechanism, especially in platform-based work. According to this book, ethical governance is essential to preventing AI from being employed as a means of invasive control and monitoring. Businesses need to make sure AI systems are applied in a way that respects the autonomy and welfare of their employees.

Additionally, according to Rudko et al. (2024), AI can support more agile procedures, decentralized decision-making, and flatter organizational structures. This calls into question established management theories and calls for fresh methods of organizational governance. This supports the main contention of the book regarding "governing in change," which holds that the impact of AI necessitates a change from conventional hierarchical control to more flexible and adaptive governance models. For ensuring that there exists alignment with organizational values and stakeholder interests, leaders will have to institute ethical use and development of AI (Benbya et al., 2020). Moral leadership in the AI era implies being proactive to prevent future hazards and ensure that AI systems are in alignment with human values.

When setting ethical regulations, the leaders need to pay attention to the effective implementation of the management of data, integrity, and data security (Lee et al.,

2023), and also to set up easily accessible, safe, and strong data governance frameworks for AI systems (Aldoseri et al., 2024).

Informational Guidelines: Give clear use case development, data governance, quality, and ethical and legal considerations top priority (Lee et al., 2023).

Transparency and Explainability: Holding systems accountable and ensuring trust depend on understanding how the decisions of AI systems are reached. Most important to the challenge of ethical AI governance is addressing the "black box" problem (Curtis et al., 2023). *Mitigation of Bias:* AI models have the ability to introduce and amplify inherent biases in data, may consolidate and amplify preexisting biases, resulting in unfair outcomes. A proactive approach is needed to identify biases and mitigate their effects in AI systems (Robert et al., 2020). *Accountability:* In cases of decisions taken using AI, lines of responsibility and accountability must be made absolutely clear (Islam & Shuford, 2024).

Human Supervision: To ensure that AI systems are used ethically and sensibly, human supervision is necessary. In this regard, Mahboub and Ghanem (2024) have shown the impact of AI on knowledge management practices and performance measurement systems.

Informational Guidelines: Give clear use case development, data governance, and quality, and ethical and legal considerations top priority (Lee et al., 2023).

In view of the above, AI leadership demands different skills and perspectives. Leaders must prioritize the ethical issues in AI development and use, as well as accelerate AI and human–AI collaboration. To understand how AI adoption has evolved over time and how its consequences are emerging over time, longitudinal studies are needed (Esmaeilzadeh, 2024; Hradecky et al., 2022).

Research Methodology and Materials

5

Abstract

This chapter presents a comprehensive research design utilized to study organizational governance model shifts in times of accelerated technological and environmental changes, from traditional HR models to AI-based frameworks. Focusing on the application of the PRISMA systematic review protocol, the study systematically screened, extracted, and reviewed 94 peer-reviewed articles from 2001 to 2025 in management, technology, and ethics journals. The study design involved rigorous screening criteria, quality assessment using CASP, and data synthesis by affinity diagramming to identify emergent themes. The key findings specify the shift toward agile governance, strategic application of AI to make organizations responsive, enabling human–AI collaboration, and addressing ethical considerations. This chapter stresses the importance of leadership, reskilling, and responsible AI governance in spurring adaptive organizational paradigms for change management in the digital era. This methodological design presents a solid foundation for building knowledge advancement and informing the usage of AI-driven organizational change.

To provide a comprehensive examination of the "Business Organization and New Organizational Models for Governing in Change: From Classical HR Models to the Role of AI," this study deployed the Preferred Reporting Items for Systematic Reviews and Meta-Analyses (PRISMA) method (Moher et al., 2009), which provides a structured framework for conducting and reporting systematic reviews. Data collection took place in early February 2025. The key steps of the PRISMA method are provided below according to (Moher et al., 2009). Below are presented the steps and protocols that were applied.

A. Rosa, *New Business Organizational Models for Governing in Times of Change*, Future of Business and Finance,
https://doi.org/10.1007/978-3-032-04091-6_5

5.1 The Key Steps of the PRISMA Method

5.1.1 Identification of Research Question

The first step involved the identification of the Research question and a clear articulation of it. The research question was framed as follows:

What are the emerging organizational models for governance in the context of change management, particularly focusing on the transition from classical HR models to the integration of artificial intelligence (AI)?

This question aims to identify gaps in the existing literature and to guide the systematic review process comprehensively.

5.1.2 Protocol Development

In the second step, protocol development was applied. A systematic review protocol was developed, outlining the following key components: Objectives: To evaluate the shift in organizational models due to the adoption of AI in HR; Inclusion and exclusion criteria; Data sources and search strategy; data extraction, and analysis methods.

5.1.3 Eligibility Criteria

In this step, inclusion and exclusion criteria were clearly established. To ensure that only the most relevant contributions were included, exclusion criteria and purification of inconsistent elements were defined.

Following a structured approach, based on the studies of Snyder (2019), parameters were applied to improve the replicability and reliability of the selection process. As highlighted by Schaefer and Alvesson (2020, p. 35), the credibility of sources plays a crucial role, distinguishing between "authority," understood as evidence to be accepted without further verification, and "source," which requires critical evaluation. Collis and Hussey (2014, p. 59) also distinguish between primary and secondary sources.

Primary sources include original information not previously explored, such as recordings or interviews, while secondary sources derive from data already collected, such as articles and reviews. In this study, types of studies, including only scientific articles and empirical research, theoretical papers, case studies, and reviews that published in peer-reviewed journals, were included to ensure the quality and comparability of the selected studies (Booth et al., 2016), while other types of publications, such as conference proceedings, book chapters, theses, working papers, and non-peer-reviewed articles and papers not written in English, were excluded from consideration given their lower impact on consolidated knowledge (Massaro et al., 2016).

5.1.4 Information Sources

In this step, database selection was done, and academic databases, including Web of Science, were used. The search was conducted in February 2025 using the Web of Science. The Web of Science (WOS) database was chosen for its broad coverage of high-impact journals and articles in the field of study, as well as for the standardization and reliability of the bibliographic data offered. The Web of Science™ database by Clarivate Analytics was also selected for its efficient data cleaning procedures (Aria and Cuccurullo, 2017).

5.1.5 Search Strategy

A key aspect of a comprehensive literature search is the accurate identification of keywords. As noted by Winchester and Salji (2016, p. 309), keywords must be closely aligned with the objective of the study, as they guide the selection of literature.

In the current study, the search process was carried out holistically, covering as many possible sources relevant to the research as were known (Collis and Hussey, 2014, p. 78).

For the research entitled "Business Organization and New Organizational Models for Governing in Change: From Classical HR Models to the Role of AI," a holistic search strategy was formulated to search for the intersection of multiple terms and their resulting keywords. The main keywords chosen were "organizational models," "governance," "HR" (human resources), "artificial intelligence," and "change management."

In order to cover an exhaustive research of the subject, synonyms and words related to each of the main keywords were added as indicated in the Table 5.1 below.

The search strategy applied Boolean operators so that these words were combined in an effective way. The major words were paired with the Boolean operator "AND" to complete all the requirements. Subtopics of every main topic were joined with the Boolean operator "OR" to widen the search and capture any possible

Table 5.1 Search strategy: the main keywords and synonyms

The main keywords	Synonyms		
"organizational models"	"organizational structures"	"business frameworks"	"management models"
"governance"	"corporate governance"	"organizational governance"	"leadership"
"HR"	"human capital management"	"personnel management"	–
"artificial intelligence"	"machine learning"	"automation"	"AI technologies"
"change management"	"organizational change"	"transformation management"	and "change leadership"

combination that fulfills at least one of the given conditions. The entire search string used here is as below (Table 5.2):

This systematic approach guarantees an in-depth analysis of the linkages between business organization, governance, human capital, artificial intelligence, and change management, so that a thorough understanding of the emerging patterns that guide organizations during periods of change is permitted.

5.1.6 Study Selection

The study selection process was conducted in two phases:

Phase 1: Title and abstract screening to identify potentially relevant studies.
Phase 2: Inspection of the whole text of promising studies to consider eligibility based on the predetermined standards.

5.1.7 Data Extraction

To pull out key data from included studies, an a priori data extraction sheet was designed, including the author(s) and year, study design and approach, sample size and details, and Key findings for adoption of AI into new organizational frameworks and HR. Data extraction was conducted with the assistance of more than one reviewer to limit error and check the quality of extracted data.

Table 5.2 The search strategy, Boolean operators, and the search string

("organizational models"	*OR*	*"organizational structures"*	*OR*	*"business frameworks"*	*OR*	*"management models")*
AND						
("governance"	*OR*	*"organizational governance"*	*OR*	*"corporate governance"*	*OR*	*"leadership")*
AND						
("HR"	*OR*	*"human resources"*	*OR*	*"personnel management")"*	*OR*	*"human capital management"*
AND						
("artificial intelligence"	*OR*	*"AI"*	*OR*	*"machine learning"*	*OR*	*"automation" OR "AI technologies")*
AND						
("change management"	*OR*	*"organizational change"*	*OR*	*"transformation management"*	*OR*	*"change leadership")*

5.1.8 Quality Evaluation

Quality appraisal is important to verify the reliability and validity of evidence employed within the review. In order to verify the methodological quality of the studies included, we employed the CASP approach. The Critical Appraisal Skills Programme (CASP) tool is a technique employed widely in determining the quality of qualitative studies in health and social care. It contains 10 questions that address different methodological issues like the specificity of research objectives, the suitability of methodology, recruitment procedures, data collection, ethical issues, and the rigor of data analysis (Hannes & Macaitis, 2012). In practice, CASP can be used to enable systematic reviews and qualitative evidence synthesis since it offers a systematic approach to evaluate the quality of the research that goes into a synthesis.

Nonetheless, its use has to be implemented with care in regard to qualitative paradigms and reporting standards of the studies under evaluation (Cochrane Qualitative and Implementation Methods Group, 2020).

Recent debate suggests that there could be some refinements in the tool, such as adding questions to assess a study's theory bases regarding clarity and consistency, to make it more relevant and useful in judging qualitative research (Thomas & Harden, 2008; APA Journal Article Reporting Standards for Qualitative Research). Generally, the CASP approach is an important aspect in augmenting qualitative research's quality assessment and, hence, its effect on evidence-based practice in the field (Sandelowski, 2006).

Next, using the CASP method with 10 quality conditions mentioned in the Table 5.3 below, each article was evaluated in terms of quality. Each article received a score from 1 to 5 in response to these conditions, and articles whose a total score

Table 5.3 CASP assessment method question specifications

Row	Question title	Question explanation
1	Research objectives	Is the selected article in line with the research direction?
2	Up-to-dateness	Is the internal information of the article up-to-date?
3	Research design	What do you think of the research design proposed in the article?
4	Sampling method	How would you evaluate the sampling method of the statistical population under study and the selected samples in this article?
5	Data collection	What is your rating of the data collection method in this article?
6	Replication	Can the points in this article be extended to other cases and used elsewhere?
7	Ethical considerations	Have the ethical principles of article writing, such as citing references, etc., been followed in this article?
8	Accuracy of data analysis	How accurate is the accuracy in data analysis?
9	Clarity of findings	How clear is the written language and the clarity of the article?
10	Research value	What is the overall value of this article?
		Assigning grades: 41–50: Excellent (E), 31–40: Very Good (VG), 21–30: Good (G), 11–20: Average (F), 0–10: Poor (P)

is 31 or higher will be approved in terms of quality, and the remaining articles will be deleted.

Then, considering the score that the articles have obtained, they will be ranked according to the following items. The CASP method evaluation table for articles is illustrated in the table below, and the table for identifying the main component in selecting approved articles is illustrated below.

Also, in this study, reliability assessment was considered to maintain the quality of the study. In qualitative research, the meaning of validity is concepts such as defensibility, believability, verifiability, and reflectability of the research results. One of the indicators of validity (reliability) of qualitative research is the evaluation of two or more documents in terms of reference to a specific indicator (Sandolowski et al., 2006).

The Kappa method is a statistical decision-making tool that examines the degree of agreement and coordination between two individuals, phenomena, or decision-making sources that have been measured separately. The Kappa coefficient is a numerical value between positive one and negative one, and the closer it is to positive one, the more direct and proportional agreement there is, and the closer it is to negative one, the more reverse and opposite agreement there is, and the values close to zero indicate disagreement.

$$k = \frac{p_o - p_e}{1 - p_e}$$

To assess reliability, a selected document was provided to one of the experts. After evaluation, the Kappa coefficient was calculated to be 0.611. A Kappa coefficient above 0.6 is desirable (Landis et al., 1977). Therefore, this value means the reliability of the research results.

5.1.9 Data Synthesis

In order to analyze and synthesize the qualitative extracted data and to enhance the depth and granularity of the analysis, the affinity diagram approach was adopted. This approach depends on sorting out individual pieces of information (here, key findings and ideas of each article) into natural categories according to their interrelationship (Islam, 2005; Iqbal et al., 2022). This approach allows for sorting out large volumes of qualitative data into sensible themes (Islam, 2005; Iqbal et al., 2022), which guarantees rich comprehension of the interrelationships among AI, organizational transformation, and governance. This enabled the identification of grand themes and sub-themes and provided a formalized structure to the analysis.

5.1.10 To Report and Dissemination

In this important step, the results of adopting the systematic review of the final-selected studies applying the PRISMA method protocol will be presented in a complete and transparent manner in order to report to the researchers, practitioners, policymakers, and other members of the scientific community. The sections of the report include results, discussion, and conclusion.

All sections are well-organized in a way to displays clarity and consistency, such that readers are able to easily see the purpose, process, and findings of the review. The report is accompanied by a PRISMA flow diagram to graphically illustrate the study selection process. Detailed results presentation reporting the systematic review result, along with qualitative analysis conducted. Results are reported using tables, figures, and a summary narrative for easy understanding. Key findings and any gaps in the literature that have been indicated are highlighted. Then, in the discussion, the implications of the findings are fully developed. This entails how the findings compare with the existing literature, how they are useful for practice, and areas of future research. Limitations of the review are also emphasized to provide a balanced view. This step is critical to make a complete and public disclosure of the results of the systematic review to be able to contribute to the body of knowledge in the field and inform evidence-based practice (Table 5.4).

In the search process, various parameters such as title, abstract, content, and article details were considered, and articles that did not match the research question and objective were eliminated. The review and selection process in this study is summarized in the Fig. 5.1 below:

Finally, after four stages of filtering, 93 studies were selected for data analysis (Tables 5.5 and 5.6) (Fig. 5.2).

The analysis of 93 final papers selected confirms the extensive field of research aiming to comprehend the intersection of AI and organizational design. The importance placed on organizational change, human resource management, and decision-making reflects the promise of change emanating from AI in transforming extant practices. In addition, the wide variety of journals reflects this research area as multidisciplinary in nature, to be of concern to management scholars and practitioners, technologists, HR professionals, and ethicists. As it becomes increasingly complicated for organizations to integrate AI, continued research will be required to inform effective models of governance as well as good behavior in this changing business organizational landscape. This section presents a detailed analysis of the 93 articles selected for this systematic review, focusing on emerging organizational models for governance in the context of change management, specifically the transition from classical HR models to the integration of artificial intelligence (AI).

Table 5.4 Research article evaluation and scoring sheet

Row	Title of article	Author	Year	Journal	Total points	Article quality grade	Confirm
1	How artificial intelligence impacts the competitive position of healthcare organizations	Ali Mohamad et al.	(2023)	*Journal of Organizational Change Management*	34	VG	Yes
2	Managing the VUCA environment: The dynamic role of organizational learning and strategic agility in B2B versus B2C firms	Atanassova et al.	(2025)	*Industrial Marketing Management*	30	G	Yes
3	How AI helps to increase organizations' capacity to manage complexity—a research perspective and solution approach bridging different disciplines	Azzam and Beckmann	(2022)	*IEEE Transactions on Engineering Management*	39	VG	Yes
4	A multilevel review of artificial intelligence in organizations: Implications for organizational behavior research and practice	Bankins et al.	(2024)	Journal of Organizational Behavior	39	VG	Yes
5	Managerial hierarchy in AI-driven organizations	Baumann and Wu	(2023)	Journal of Organization Design	34	VG	Yes
6	Artificial intelligence in organizations: Current state and future opportunities	Benbya et al.	(2020)	MIS Quarterly	32	VG	Yes
7	What a difference a word makes: Understanding threats to performance in a VUCA world	Bennett and Lemoine	(2014)	Business horizons	24	G	Yes
8	Barriers to the Implementation of AI in Organizations: Findings from a Delphi Study	Bérubé et al.	(2021)	Hawaii International Conference on System Sciences	18	F	NO
9	Decision-making in organizations: Should managers use AI?	Brink et al.	(2024)	Journal of Business Strategy	32	VG	Yes
10	Understanding managers' attitudes and behavioral intentions towards using artificial intelligence for organizational decision-making	Cao et al.	(2021)	Technovation	31	VG	Yes
11	Corporate Foresight: Navigating Uncertainty in a VUCA World	Carayannis et al.	(2025)	*J Knowl Econ*	24	G	Yes

12	Adaptive Leadership: Thriving in Times of Uncertainty	Chaudhry et al.	(2024)	*Center for Management Science Research*	14	F	NO
13	AI-Driven Organizational Culture Evolution: A Critical Review	Chourasia et al.	(2024)	International Conference on Communication, Computer Sciences and Engineering (IC3SE), IEEE	15	F	NO
14	Artificial intelligence for the real world	Davenport and Ronanki	(2018)	Harvard business review	14	F	NO
15	The impact of artificial intelligence on organizations and managers: The skills needed for an effective leadership	Di Prima et al.	(2024)	Artificial Intelligence and Business Transformation. Springer, Chapter	17	F	NO
16	AI-driven organizational change: Transforming structures and processes in the modern workplace	Elkahlout et al.	(2024)	International Journal of Academic Information Systems Research (IJAISR)	32	VG	Yes
17	Crafting a winning workplace culture: Understanding organizational dynamics using AI tools	Ghannam	(2025)	Building Business Knowledge for Complex Modern Business Environments. IGI Global. Book.	18	F	NO
18	The empowerment of artificial intelligence in post-digital organizations: Exploring human interactions with supervisory AI	Gladden et al.	(2022)	Human Technology	32	VG	Yes
19	Exploring artificial intelligence adoption in public organizations: A comparative case study	Neumann et al.	(2024)	Public Management Review	30	G	Yes
20	Organizational agility, visionary leadership in the age of VUCA	Friedman	(2020)	Available at SSRN	17	F	NO
21	Artificial intelligence: An overview of research trends and future directions	Gursoy and Cai	(2025)	International journal of contemporary hospitality management	29	G	Yes
22	Long problems: Climate change and the challenge of governing across time	Hale	(2024)	Princeton University Press. Book.	15	F	NO

(continued)

Table 5.4 (continued)

Row	Title of article	Author	Year	Journal	Total points	Article quality grade	Confirm
23	Management of Organizational Change: Leveraging Transformation	Harigopal	(2006)	SAGE Publications India. Book.	14	F	NO
24	How organizations can innovate with generative AI	Holmström and Carroll	(2024)	Business Horizons	32	VG	*Yes*
25	Embracing resilience in pharmaceutical manufacturing: "digital twins"–forging a resilient path in the VUCA maze	Joseph	(2025)	*International Journal of Pharmaceutical and Healthcare Marketing*	24	G	Yes
26	Organization design: Current insights and future research directions	Joseph and Sengul	(2025)	*Journal of Management*	24	G	Yes
27	Partnering with AI: How organizations can win over skeptical managers	Kolbjørnsrud et al.	(2017)	Strategy & Leadership	29	G	Yes
28	Change: How organizations achieve hard-to-imagine results in uncertain and volatile times	Kotter	(2025)	John Wiley & Sons,Book.	17	F	NO
29	Exploring the factors, affordances and constraints outlining the implementation of Artificial Intelligence in public sector organizations	Maragno et al.	(2023)	International Journal of Information Management	30	G	*Yes*
30	Applications of Leadership Theories and Concepts in Environmental Leadership	Miao and Nduneseokwu	(2024)	Environmental Leadership in a VUCA Era. Springer, Chapter	16	F	NO
31	The threat of offensive AI to organizations	Mirsky et al.	(2023)	Computers & Security	29	G	Yes
32	Artificial intelligence and knowledge sharing: Contributing factors to organizational performance	Olan et al.	(2022)	Journal of Business Research	27	G	Yes
33	The potential of generative artificial intelligence across disciplines: Perspectives and future directions	Ooi et al.	(2023)	*Journal of Computer Information Systems*	26	G	Yes
34	Management toward Industry 5.0: a co-worker ship approach on digital transformation for future innovative manufacturing	Olsson et al.	(2025)	European Journal of Innovation Management	24	G	Yes

35	Responsible artificial intelligence governance: A review and research framework	Papagiannidis et al.	(2025)	The Journal of Strategic Information Systems	31	VG	Yes
36	Adoption of artificial intelligence (AI) for talent acquisition in IT/ITeS organizations	Pillai and Sivathanu	(2020)	Benchmarking: An International Journal	24	G	Yes
37	Artificial intelligence and management: The automation–augmentation paradox	Raisch, S., and Krakowski	(2021)	*Academy of management review*	29	G	Yes
38	Combining human and artificial intelligence: Hybrid problem-solving in organizations	Raisch, and Fomina	(2023)	*Academy of Management Review*	35	VG	Yes
39	How does AI-enabled HR analytics influence employee resilience: job crafting as a mediator and HRM system strength as a moderator?	Xiao et al.	(2025)	*Personnel Review*	40	VG	Yes
40	New institutional theory and AI: toward rethinking of artificial intelligence in organizations	Rudko et al.	(2024)	*Journal of Management History*	42	E	Yes
41	Artificial intelligence and the end of bounded rationality: A new era in organizational decision making	Shick et al.	(2024)	*Development and Learning in Organizations: An International Journal*	32	VG	Yes
42	Organizational decision-making structures in the age of artificial intelligence	Shrestha et al.	(2019)	California management review	31	VG	Yes
43	Clarifying the conceptual map of VUCA: a systematic review	Taskan et al.	(2022)	*International Journal of Organizational Analysis*	24	G	Yes
44	New way out of efficiency-equity dilemma: Digital technology empowerment for local government environmental governance	Wang and Guo	(2024)	Technological Forecasting and Social Change	31	VG	Yes
45	AI–human interaction in the workplace: Navigating dynamics and impact	Abujarour et al.	(2024)	*SaudiCIS 2024 Proceedings.* 74.	14	F	NO
46	The great debate-can AI and automation lead to More Or Fewer Jobs	Challoumis	(2024)	*XIX International Scientific Conference. London. Great Britain*	14	F	NO
47	In the hearts and minds of employees: A model of pre-adoptive appraisal toward artificial intelligence in organizations	Chiu et al.	(2021)	*International Journal of Information Management*	36	VG	Yes

(continued)

Table 5.4 (continued)

Row	Title of article	Author	Year	Journal	Total points	Article quality grade	Confirm
48	How AI tools can—and cannot—help organizations become more ethical	De Cremer and Narayanan	(2023)	Frontiers in Artificial Intelligence	35	VG	Yes
49	On the juggernaut of artificial intelligence in organizations, research and society	Gendron et al.	(2024)	Critical Perspectives on Accounting	32	VG	Yes
50	Rebooting employees: Upskilling for artificial intelligence in multinational corporations	Jaiswal et al.	(2023)	*Artificial Intelligence and International HRM*, Chapter	17	F	NO
51	Reconfiguring digital embeddedness in hybrid work: The case of employee experience management platforms	John et al.	(2024)	*Information Systems Journal*	31	VG	Yes
52	Designing fair AI for managing employees in organizations: A review, critique, and design agenda	Robert et al.	(2020)	Human–Computer Interaction	34	VG	Yes
53	The implementation of artificial intelligence in organizations: A systematic literature review	Lee et al.	(2023)	Information and Management	33	VG	Yes
54	Examining how AI capabilities can foster organizational performance in public organizations	Mikalef et al.	(2023)	Government Information Quarterly	33	VG	Yes
55	Enhancing employee performance through AIenabled HR analytics: Exploring the roles of job crafting, perceived risk, and employee engagement	Bagis and Yulianeu	(2024)	*Journal of Digitovation and Information System*	42	VG	Yes
56	Implications of artificial intelligence on organizational agility: A PLS-SEM and PLS-POS approach	Ştefan et al.	(2024)	Amfiteatru Economic	42	VG	Yes
57	Integrating AI in organizations for value creation through HumanAI teaming: A dynamic-capabilities approach	Simón et al.	(2024)	*Journal of Business Research*	42	VG	Yes

58	Artificial intelligence in human resource management: Objectives and implications	Tursunbayeva et al.	(2023)	Impact of Artificial Intelligence in Business and Society. Opportunities and Challenges. Routledge. Book	15	F	NO
59	Crafting a job: Revisioning employees as active crafters of their work	Wrzesniewski, and Dutton	(2001)	*Academy of management review*	40	VG	Yes
60	Towards adoption of generative AI in organizational settings	Prasad Agrawal	(2024)	Journal of Computer Information Systems	42	VG	Yes
61	Methodological approach to assessing the current state of organizations for AI-based digital transformation	Aldoseri et al.	(2024)	Applied System Innovation	42	VG	Yes
62	AI-deploying organizations are key to addressing 'perfect storm' of AI risks	Curtis et al.	(2023)	AI Ethics	35	VG	Yes
63	Challenges and strategies for wide-scale artificial intelligence (AI) deployment in healthcare practices: A perspective for healthcare organizations	Esmaeilzadeh	(2024)	*Artificial Intelligence in Medicine*	30	G	Yes
64	Towards an ethical and inclusive implementation of artificial intelligence in organizations: a multidimensional framework	Hernández et al.	(2024)	arXiv preprint arXiv:2405.01697.	18	F	NO
65	Organizational readiness to adopt artificial intelligence in the exhibition sector in Western Europe	Hradecky et al.	(2022)	*International journal of information management*	36	VG	Yes
66	Artificial intelligence: A strategy to harness its power through organizational learning	Jarrahi et al.	(2023)	Journal of Business Strategy	40	VG	Yes
67	Ready or not, AI comes—an interview study of organizational AI readiness factors	Jöhnk et al.	(2021)	*Business & Information Systems Engineering*	36	VG	Yes
68	Quantitative Assessment on Investigation on the Impact of Artificial Intelligence on HR Practices and Organizational Efficiency for Industry 4.0	Kulshrestha	(2024)	*Journal of Artificial Intelligence, Machine Learning and Neural Network*	42	E	Yes

(continued)

Table 5.4 (continued)

Row	Title of article	Author	Year	Journal	Total points	Article quality grade	Confirm
69	State-of-the-art analysis of adopting AI-based conversational agents in organizations: A systematic literature review	Lewandowski et al.	(2021)	PACIS	39	VG	Yes
70	A framework to overcome challenges to the adoption of artificial intelligence in Indian Government Organizations	Misra et al.	(2023)	*Technological Forecasting and Social Change*	40	VG	Yes
71	Implementing AI in organizations: The role of leaders and its impact on leadership	Ressem	(2023)	(Master's thesis, NTNU)	14	F	NO
72	Shaping Tomorrow's Workplace with AI-Driven HRM: Bridging the gap between technology and human capital	Sainila	(2024)	Master's thesis	15	F	NO
73	Adoption of AI by the HR function in the civil service	Smith et al.	(2024)	*Employee Relations: The International Journal*	42	E	Yes
74	Who picks up the errors of artificial intelligence? Case Study	Vaccaro et al.	(2025)	IESE Business School	18	F	NO
75	AI And Creativity: How Business Can Add Ethics to Decision-Making?	Vaccaro and Fioravante	(2025)	Forbes	18	F	NO
76	Factors inhibiting the adoption of artificial intelligence at organizational-level: A preliminary investigation	Alsheiabni	(2019)	*Americas Conference on Information Systems 2019* Association for Information Systems	17	F	NO
77	Personalism in generative AI deployment: Deciding ethically when human creative expression is at stake	Fioravante and Vaccaro	(2024)	Humanistic Management Journal	35	VG	Yes
78	A survey of ethical considerations in AI: navigating the landscape of bias and fairness	Islam and Shuford	(2024)	*Journal of Artificial Intelligence General Science (JAIGS)*	35	VG	Yes

79	Factors influencing the AI adoption in organizations	Kurup and Gupta	(2022)	Metamorphosis	32	VG	Yes
80	The mediating role of knowledge management practices and balanced scorecard in the association between artificial intelligence and organization performance: Evidence from MENA region commercial banks	Mahboub and Ghanem	(2024)	*Cogent Business & Management*	34	VG	Yes
81	Putting AI into context-method support for the introduction of artificial intelligence into organizations	Sandkuhl	(2019)	2019 IEEE 21st Conference on Business Informatics (CBI)	15	F	NO
82	Unfreezing change as three steps: Rethinking Kurt Lewin's legacy for change management	Cummings et al.	(2016)	Human Relations	29	G	Yes
83	Antecedents of generative artificial intelligence technology adoption: Extended innovation of diffusion model with cultural dimensions and risks perceptions	Alamri	(2025)	*Journal of Ecohumanism*	39	VG	Yes
84	Adoption of artificial intelligence in human resource management	Kaur et al.	(2021)	*Indian Journal of Industrial Relation*	29	G	Yes
85	Barriers and enablers of AI adoption in human resource management: A critical analysis of organizational and technological factors	Madanchian and Taherdoost	(2025)	*Information*	39	VG	Yes
86	Operations research in the context of AI applications.	Lemos Sic	(2022)	Annals of Operations Research	39	VG	Yes
87	AI adoption in enterprises for enhanced strategic human resource management practices: Benefiting the employee engagement and experience	Alzeiby et al.	(2025)	*Journal of Enterprise Information Management*	35	G	Yes
88	Exploring the role of leadership in strategic change: A global perspective	Popli and Rizvi	(2016)	Global Business Review	33	VG	Yes
89	Customer relationship management and customer value creation	Storbacka and Nenonen	(2009)	European Journal of Marketing	29	G	Yes
90	Technological innovation and firm performance in emerging markets	Tohanean et al.	(2020)	Amfiteatru Economic	35	VG	Yes

(continued)

Table 5.4 (continued)

Row	Title of article	Author	Year	Journal	Total points	Article quality grade	Confirm
91	Factors influencing the adoption of artificial intelligence in organizations–from an employee's perspective	Ambati	(2020)	Conference: MWAIS 2020 Proceedings.	16	F	NO
92	Managing artificial intelligence	Berente et al.	(2021)	MIS Quarterly	27	G	Yes
93	The role of predictive analytics in organizational change management	Cate	(2025)	researchgate.net	17	F	NO
94	Artificial intelligence and predictive analytics: Revolutionizing strategic business insights in digital era	Georgewill and Gabriel	(2024)	5th International Academic Conference Proceedings,	18	F	NO
95	The European railway sectors: Understanding and assessing change	ESPOSITO	(2017)	Departmental Working Papers. Università degli Studi di Milano.	15	F	NO
96	AI and change management	Hechler et al.	(2020)	Deploying AI in the Enterprise. Apress, Berkeley, CA. Book.	16	F	NO
97	Reclaiming the education doctorate: Three cases of processes and roles in institutional change	Perry	(2010)	University of Maryland, College Park.	14	F	NO
98	Change management in the public sector: The use of cross-functional teams	Piercy et al.	(2013)	Production Planning & Control	24	G	Yes
99	Successful organizational change: Integrating the management practice and scholarly literatures	Stouten et al.	(2018)	*Academy of Management Annals*	26	G	Yes
100	On the current state of combining human and artificial intelligence for strategic organizational decision making	Trunk et al.	(2020)	*Business Research*	43	E	Yes
101	Artificial intelligence in human resources management: Challenges and a path forward	Tambe et al.	(2019)	*California Management Review*	42	E	Yes

102	Examining the effect of organizational leadership,organizational structure, and employee technological capability on the success of electronic human resource management	Amoako et al.	(2022)	*SAGE Open*	27	G	Yes
103	Digitalization and performance management: A conceptual framework for HR governance	Samir	(2024)	Journal of Economics, Finance and Management (JEFM)	30	G	Yes
104	Effects of technology and digital innovations on the human resources ecosystem	Al-Alawi et al.	(2021)	International conference on decision aid sciences and application (DASA), IEEE.	16	F	NO
105	AI adoption in healthcare: Addressing challenges and change management	Leuba and Piricz	(2024)	*IEEE 24th International Symposium on Computational Intelligence and Informatics*	18	F	NO
106	Transformative human resources: Mapping future directions for innovation in information technology and multidisciplinary applications	Maria and Susan	(2024)	*2nd International Conference on Technology Innovation and Its Applications (ICTIIA)*	17	F	NO
107	Keeping the organization in the loop: a socio-technical extension of human-centered artificial intelligence	Herrmann and Pfeiffer	(2023)	*AI & Soc*	36	VG	Yes
108	Application of artificial intelligence in enterprise human resource management and employee performance evaluation	Nie	(2024)	*International Journal of Computer Applications in Technology*	43	E	Yes
109	Intelligent human resources for the adoption of artificial intelligence: a systematic literature review	Jatobá et al.	(2023)	*Journal of Organizational Change Management*	30	G	Yes
110	Human resource management in the digital era	Singhraul and Anuragi	(2024)	*International Journal of Research in Commerce and Management Studies (IJRCMS)*	40	VG	Yes
111	The mediating effect of leadership in artificial intelligence success for employee-engagement	Divya et al.	(2024)	*Management Decision*	42	E	Yes
112	AI-driven HR transformation in Chinese automotive industry: strategies and implications	Khushik et al.	(2025)	*Business Process Management Journal*	40	VG	Yes

(continued)

Table 5.4 (continued)

Row	Title of article	Author	Year	Journal	Total points	Article quality grade	Confirm
113	The impact of digital transformation on formal and informal organizational structures of large architecture and engineering firms	Bonanomi et al.	(2020)	*Engineering, Construction and Architectural Management*	24	G	Yes
114	HR in the digital age: How digital technology will change HR's organization structure, processes and roles	DiRomualdo et al.	(2018)	*Strategic HR Review*	32	VG	Yes
115	Exploring organizational change in the age of digital transformation and its impact on talent management: Trends and challenges	Montero Guerra and Danvila-Del	(2024)	*Journal of Organizational Change Management*	36	VG	Yes
116	Transforming HR into a strategic partner: A case study of organizational redesign for sustainable growth	Douglas and Haley	(2025)	*Strategic HR Review*	35	VG	Yes
117	Artificial intelligence and participatory leadership: The role of technological transformation in business management and its impact on employee participation	Sarioguz and Miser	(2024)	*International Research Journal of Modernization in Engineering, Technology and Science*	39	VG	Yes
118	The future of leadership—How is leadership in small and medium-sized enterprises going to change?	Ötting et al.	(2021)	*Gr Interakt Org*	26	G	Yes
119	Change management towards good university governance in Indonesia	Fatmawati et al.	(2024)	*Cogent Social Sciences*	28	G	Yes
120	Transformational and transactional leaders and their role in implementing the Kotter Change Management Model Ensuring ensuring sustainable change: An empirical study	Mouazen et al.	(2024)	*Sustainability*	29	G	Yes

121	Key factors in organizational change: Case studies of Netflix and FinoTechno Change Management Models	Zheng	(2024)	*Advances in Economics, Management and Political Sciences*	38	VG	Yes
122	Maximizing employee engagement through artificial intelligent organizational culture in the context of leadership and training of employees: Testing linear and nonlinear relationships	Rožman et al.	(2023)	*Cogent Business & Management*	42	E	Yes
123	Transformative AI in human resource management: Enhancing workforce planning with topic modeling	Venugopal et al.	(2024)	*Cogent Business & Management*	40	VG	Yes
124	The autonomy tussle: AI technology and employee job crafting responses	Perez et al.	(2022)	*Relations industrielles/ Industrial Relations*	39	VG	Yes

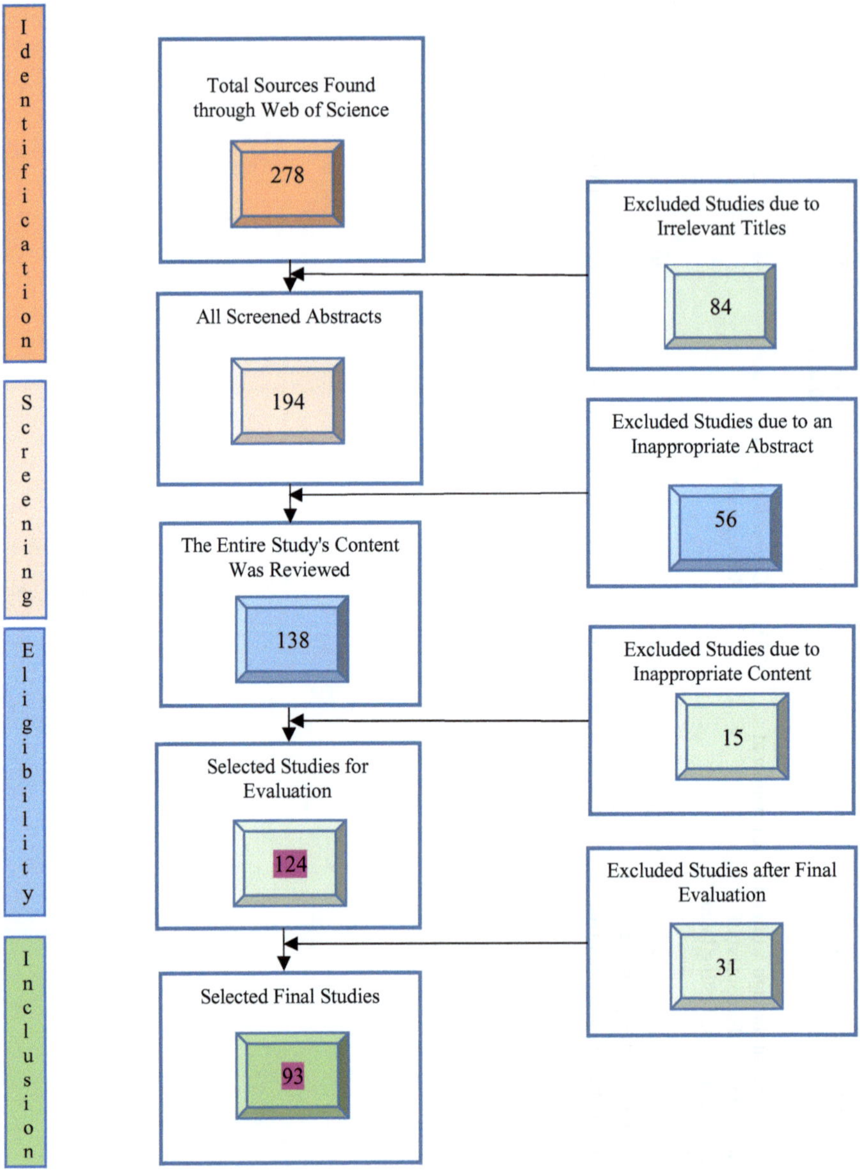

Fig. 5.1 The PRISMA flow diagram

Table 5.5 Distribution of selected articles by journal

Journal	Frequency
Journal of Organizational Change Management	4
International journal of information management	3
Cogent Business & Management	3
Academy of management review	3
Strategic HR Review	2
Journal of Business Research	2
Journal of Business Strategy	2
California Management Review	2
MIS Quarterly	2
Amfiteatru Economic	2
Technological Forecasting and Social Change	2
Journal of Computer Information Systems	2
Business horizons	1
Humanistic Management Journal	1
Business Process Management Journal	1
Business Research	1
Journal of Enterprise Information Management	1
Cogent Social Sciences	1
Advances in Economics, Management and Political Sciences	1
Sustainability	1
Journal of Management	1
Journal of Management History	1
International Journal of Computer Applications in Technology	1
Management Decision	1
International Journal of Research in Commerce and Management Studies	1
Gr Interakt Org	1
Engineering, Construction and Architectural Management	1
AI & Soc	1
SAGE Open	1
Journal of Economics, Finance and Management (JEFM)	1
Academy of Management Annals	1
Production Planning & Control	1
Industrial Marketing Management	1
Global Business Review	1
IEEE Transactions on Engineering Management	1
Journal of Organizational Behavior	1
European Journal of Innovation Management	1
European Journal of Marketing	1
Indian Journal of Industrial Relation	1
Annals of Operations Research	1

(continued)

Table 5.5 (continued)

Journal	Frequency
Information	1
Government Information Quarterly	1
Human Relations	1
Journal of Ecohumanism	1
Journal of Artificial Intelligence General Science (JAIGS)	1
Business & Information Systems Engineering	1
Employee Relations: The International Journal	1
Information and Management	1
Journal of Artificial Intelligence, Machine Learning and Neural Network	1
Artificial Intelligence in Medicine	1
Applied System Innovation	1
Human–Computer Interaction	1
Journal of Organization Design	1
PACIS	1
Metamorphosis	1
Information Systems Journal	1
Technovation	1
AI Ethics	1
J Knowl Econ	1
International Journal of Academic Information Systems Research	1
Frontiers in Artificial Intelligence	1
Critical Perspectives on Accounting	1
International Journal of Organizational Analysis	1
Human Technology	1
Development and Learning in Organizations: An International Journal	1
Benchmarking: An International Journal	1
The Journal of Strategic Information Systems	1
Computers & Security	1
Strategy & Leadership	1
International journal of contemporary hospitality management	1
Public Management Review	1
Relations industrielles/Industrial Relations	1
International Journal of Pharmaceutical and Healthcare Marketing	1
Total number	93

Table 5.6 Distribution of selected articles by year of publication

Publication year	Frequency
(2024)	31
(2023)	16
(2025)	10
(2022)	8
(2021)	6
(2020)	6
(2019)	3
(2018)	2
(2016)	2
(2017)	1
(2015)	1
(2014)	1
(2013)	1
(2012)	1
(2009)	1
(2004)	1
(2001)	1
Total number	93

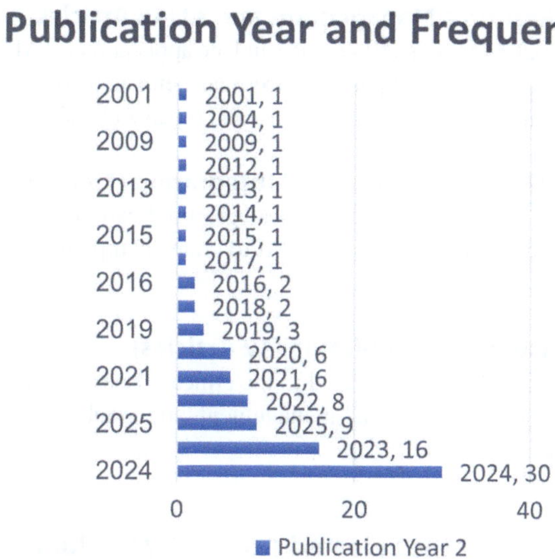

Fig. 5.2 Distribution of selected articles by year of publication

5.2 Results of the SLR

5.2.1 Distribution of the Selected Articles by the Main Topic

The analyzed articles can be categorized into several main topics reflecting their focus on various aspects of business organization and the integration of artificial intelligence (AI) in organizational models. The following categories emerged from a review of the articles:

5.2.1.1 Artificial Intelligence for Decision-Making (20 Articles)

A considerable percentage of articles (22%) discuss the use of AI to improve decision-making in organizations. These articles discuss how AI can enable improved decision-making, enhance organizational responsiveness, and manage management complexities.

5.2.1.2 Organizational Change and Transformation (25 Articles)

This is the 28% category of articles that discusses the larger organizational implications of AI on change. These are topics such as AI-led transformations, how digital transformation affects organizational design, and managing change in a VUCA world.

5.2.1.3 Human Resource Management and AI (18 Articles)

Some 20% of the articles focus on HR practice and the applications of AI to talent acquisition, employee engagement, and performance management. This mirrors increasing recognition of how AI can support HR functions and organizational efficiency.

5.2.1.4 Strategic Management and AI Integration (15 Articles)

Around 17% of the articles examine the strategic implications of AI in organizations, including frameworks for leveraging AI to create competitive advantages and improve overall performance.

5.2.1.5 Ethical Issues and Regulation (12 Articles)

Around 13% of the articles are dedicated to the ethical issues AI raises in organizational life and the need for ethical management and establishing structures to address these issues (Fig. 5.3).

5.2.2 Distribution of the Selected Articles by the Journal Topic

The articles were published in a variety of academic journals, each with its own thematic leanings, which suggests a multidisciplinary approach to studying AI in organizational contexts. The distribution is outlined below:

5.2.2.1 Organizational Change and Management Journals (35 Articles)

Most articles (39%) have been published in journals with concern regarding managing, organizational change, and behavior, reflecting high concern with the ways in which AI is altering conventional methods of managing.

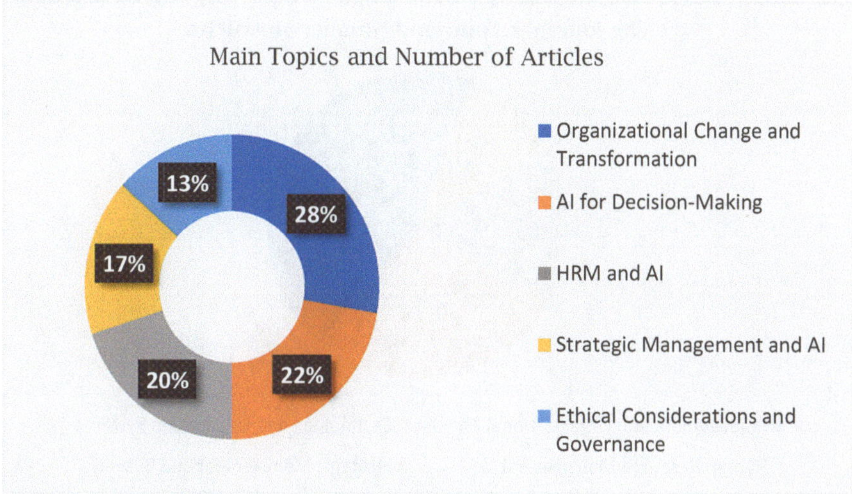

Fig. 5.3 Distribution of the selected articles by the main topic

5.2.2.2 Technology and Information Systems Journals (25 Articles)

Almost 28% of the final selected studies were displayed in technology-oriented journals, were interested in the organizational domain, and technological innovations. These kinds of journals are more intended to discover the junction at which data management, AI, and organizational performance meet.

5.2.2.3 HRM Journals (15 Articles)

About 17% of the contributions were released in HR-specialized journals, which highlighted introducing AI into the operations of HR and the digital age new HR dynamic.

5.2.2.4 Business and Strategic Management Journals (10 Articles)

Around 11% of the articles were featured in strategic management journals, reflecting a focus on competitive strategy and the role of AI in shaping organizational strategies.

5.2.2.5 Governance and Ethics Journals (5 Articles)

Only 5% of the articles were published in journals specifically dedicated to ethics and governance, reflecting greater awareness of the need to respond to ethical concerns in the deployment of AI technology (Fig. 5.4).

5.2.3 Article Description and Categorization Data Synthesis

In this section, a list of the final 93 selected studies, along with a brief description and categorization based on the identified themes, is presented. Through the extensive literature review and by adopting the affinity diagram, which facilitated the identification

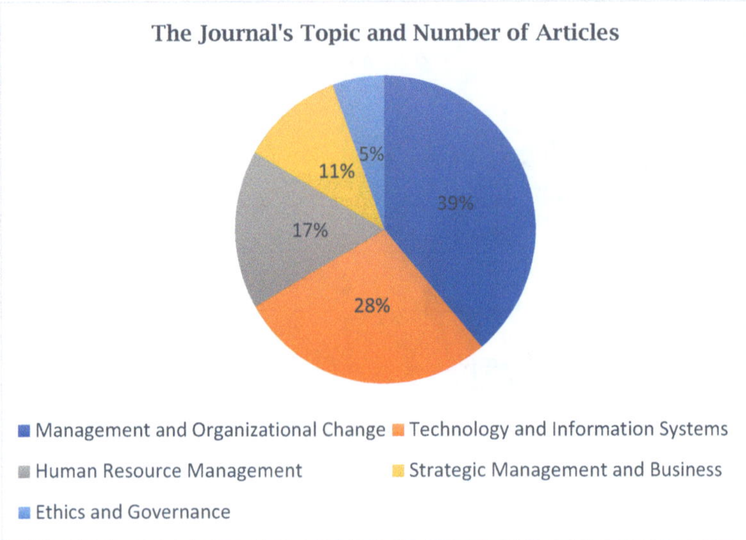

Fig. 5.4 Distribution of the selected articles by the journal's topic and number of articles

of key patterns and relationships, the articles' contents and research findings were categorized, and after that, several key themes emerged that relate to the research question regarding the transformation of organizational governance in the age of AI.

5.2.3.1 Theme 1: Evolution from Traditional Structure to Agile Governance Models

Literature is an ongoing call for organizations to create responsive governance frameworks that are in a position to react in a timely manner to fast-changing environmental demands.

Studies by Atanassova et al. (2025) and Elkahlout et al. (2024) concentrate on this trend, demonstrating how companies are adopting more and more agility to counter the frailties of the VUCA era. To illustrate, studies on agile decision-making processes and adaptive organizations in organizational learning and strategic agility ascertain flexible organizations and adaptive decision-making processes that enable rapid response to external disturbances. In addition, new technologies like artificial intelligence (AI) are transforming organizational decision-making models, also fostering decentralized and responsive governance models (Shrestha et al., 2019).

All this change also calls for a revisit of historical organizational design principles, with modern structures now tending toward modularity, networking, and matrix forms to become more flexible. As Joseph and Sengul (2025) observe, organizational design currently focuses on building innovation and resilience using adaptive governance structures. Leadership also has an important role to play in this change, with transformational and adaptive leadership being key in developing and maintaining agile governance structures (Mouazen et al., 2024).

As a whole, the move toward agile models from the classical bureaucratic governance is an inevitable reaction to the needs of a complicated, high-speed world.

5.2.3.2 Theme 2: AI and Organizational Agility:

Organizations use AI applications to empower predictive analysis, real-time tracking of data (Benbya et al., 2020; Gursoy and Cai, 2025). The ability that they provide organizations with to use evidence-based decisions makes efficacy feasible, thus improved responsiveness and resilience. Also, AI-driven data allows organizations to foster continuous improvement by identifying trends. As mentioned by scholars, the adoption of AI besides improving also promotes the structural and evolutionary necessary for effective action in uncertain environments (Azzam et al., 2022; Elkahlout et al., 2024; Ştefan et al., 2024)

5.2.3.3 Theme 3: Human–AI Interaction (Human–AI Collaboration)

Current research highlights the importance of developing common platforms based on the deepening convergence of AI capabilities with human competencies. At the center of such an approach is the imperative of the coordination between machine and human intelligence in order to enable both resources to work synergistically and propel organizational performance. Strong leadership in the AI era is based on human-centered approaches that leverage the complementarities of human and AI systems. Building up workflows that produce seamless human–AI collaboration is imperative because this results in increased creativity and problem-solving ability (Bankins et al., 2024; Gladden et al., 2022).

Studies have indicated possible hybrid problem-solving organizational structures in which human intuition and AI-facilitated intelligence are combined to address complex challenges (Raisch & Fomina, 2023). Second, human and artificial intelligence decision-making at the strategic level must be carried out with precise regard for socio-technical aspects to ensure the AI systems are always aligned with human values and organizational objectives (Herrmann & Pfeiffer, 2023).

5.2.3.4 Theme 4: AI Ethics and Governance

Ethical AI deployment in business remains a priority area, and studies are being conducted that further highlight the necessity of putting good foundations in place for AI use governance. These values work toward increasing transparency, decreasing prejudices, and upholding organizational responsibility, and hence human dignity in decision-making (Robert et al., 2020; Papagiannidis et al., 2025).

Organizations are heavily accountable for actively monitoring these ethical issues, putting governance structures in place that monitor AI adoption and restrict related risks. Not just strict compliance with prevailing ethical standards, but an ongoing ethical culture of inquiry and responsibility. Organization leadership, Curtis et al. (2023) remark, has an imperative role to answer the 'perfect storm' of threats posed by AI, to ensure social values and ethical norms are upheld for AI technologies. Apart from that, the capacity of AI to enhance organizational ethics must be weighed against its limitations.

De Cremer and Narayanan (2023) discuss both the strengths and weaknesses of AI technology for enhancing ethical behavior in organizations. Furthermore, ethical concerns involving human creativity and expression are gaining importance as Fioravante and Vaccaro (2024) also describe in relation to generative AI, underscoring the need for ethical decision-making whenever AI impacts human creative outputs.

It is important to have a full understanding of the issues because Islam and Shuford (2024) chart the terrain of bias and fairness in AI. There must be effective governance policies and ethical frameworks established for a proper structure that ensures AI systems are working for good in society ethically and responsibly.

5.2.3.5 Theme 5: Transformational Leadership and AI

Transformational leadership of authenticity basing itself on transparency, moral character, and genuine participation is particularly important in leading organizations through post linearity of AI deployment and integration (Agrawal, 2024; Shick et al., 2024).New models of decision-making require leadership to transform in response. For example, Brink et al. (2024) mention the significance of AI environment manager decision-making by stating that strong leaders are those who know when and how to use AI tools in a manner to maximize organizational performance. Likewise, Cao et al. (2021) discuss managers' attitude and behavioral intention to implement AI, mentioning further that positive attitudes and leadership support are of great importance in successful AI adoption.

Securing buy-in from the managers is still a major challenge. Kolbjørnsrud et al. (2017) explain how one can convince hesitant managers to embrace AI, with a focus on showing value and connecting AI initiatives with business objectives. Divya et al. (2024) also highlight the leadership mediating role in explaining the involvement of good leadership in the success of AI and employee engagement, and propose that transformational leaders can create a culture of trust to incubate innovation so that AI can be maximally utilized.

In addition to that, the convergence of participatory leadership strategies with AI positions technological change as the bedrock to boost employees' empowerment and participation (Sarioguz & Miser, 2024). Such tactics democratize decision-making, encouraging teamwork and shared responsibility rather than AI-based projects.

The influence of AI is most pronounced in the organizational structures of SMEs. Ötting et al. (2021) explain how AI is transforming leadership in such firms to the extent that attention is being given to more participative, responsive, and adaptive leadership patterns as aligned with the changing technology environment.

Ultimately, it requires deliberate leadership and training to create an AI-culture organizational environment maximized for employee empowerment. Rožman et al. (2023) elaborate on the dynamic interplays among learning, leadership, and employee engagement, showing how effective leadership and continuous learning can realize lasting, innovative, and committed workforces that are able to function in AI-enabled environments.

5.2.3.6 Theme 6: Reskilling and Workforce Adaptation (HR and Workforce)

To handle AI-fueled transformation well, companies must make investments in continuous reskilling and upskilling programs. All the literature suggests that workers need to be supported in building their new skills so that they can maintain the momentum in the evolving world established because of artificial intelligence. Through investments in continuous learning programs, organizations can make their employees work in conjunction with AI technologies seamlessly, increasing organizational resilience and agility (Rudko et al., 2024; Mikalef et al., 2023).

Research offers a number of dimensions to this adaptation process. For example, organizational readiness factors shaping AI integration are determined by Jöhnk et al. (2021), with the imperative of building a skilled and dynamic labor force. Likewise, Kulshrestha (2024) offers quantitative evidence for the effect of AI on HR practice and business efficiency, attesting to the necessity for focused reskilling in order to derive full benefit. The use of AI technologies by HR functions, such as conversational agents (Lewandowski et al., 2021) and electronic human resource management systems (Amoako et al., 2022), also identifies the learning of technology skills on the part of employees.

Besides this, digital transformation is also transforming talent management and performance assessment processes (Singhraul & Anuragi, 2024; Nie, 2024). As organizations reengineer work jobs from active job creators of employees (Wrzesniewski & Dutton, 2001) to change leaders (Montero Guerra & Danvila-Del, 2024) reskilling is part of providing workforce pertinence. Tools such as AI workforce planning (Venugopal et al., 2024; Khushk et al., 2025) demonstrate the myriad complexities involved in creating a dynamic, future-proofed workforce. In general, long-term reskilling and labor adjustment are forces to leverage the full potential of AI. Businesses investing intentionally in employee development will gain more in the digital economy with effortless transfer of labor and ongoing organizational performance.

5.2.3.7 Theme 7: AI Deployment and Adoption (AI Implementation)

The successful deployment and use of AI in organizations are dependent on various determinative factors that include organizational readiness, strategic adoption practices, and adequate management of adoption hurdles.

Organization readiness to adopt AI is crucial. Understanding the employees, technology architecture, and support from leadership shapes AI adoption readiness. As an example, Chiu (2021) highlights the necessity of understanding employees' pre-adoption attitudes as a success factor in AI. Likewise, Hradecky et al. (2022) also examine industry readiness, with a special focus on industry-specific strategies for industries.

Effective AI deployment is a matter of setting the right strategies. Agrawal (2024) provides strategic frameworks for the deployment of generative AI through a phased approach, stakeholders, and continuous evaluation. Rudko et al. (2024) also propose institutional theories to remake AI adoption processes to fit organizational goals and legitimacy. Lee et al. (2023) also provide a systematic review of AI implementation practices, citing best practices including embedding AI in workflows and supporting an innovation culture.

Various challenges confront organizations, ranging from technical complexity to moral issues and opposition. Esmaeilzadeh (2024) has insights for healthcare environments, offering methods such as comprehensive training and stakeholder engagement in conquering challenges. Misra (2023) provides a model for Indian government agencies, with policy support and capacity building as major highlights. In addition, Mahboub and Ghanem (2024) also highlight the mediating role of knowledge management practices and balanced scorecards in enhancing the impact of AI on

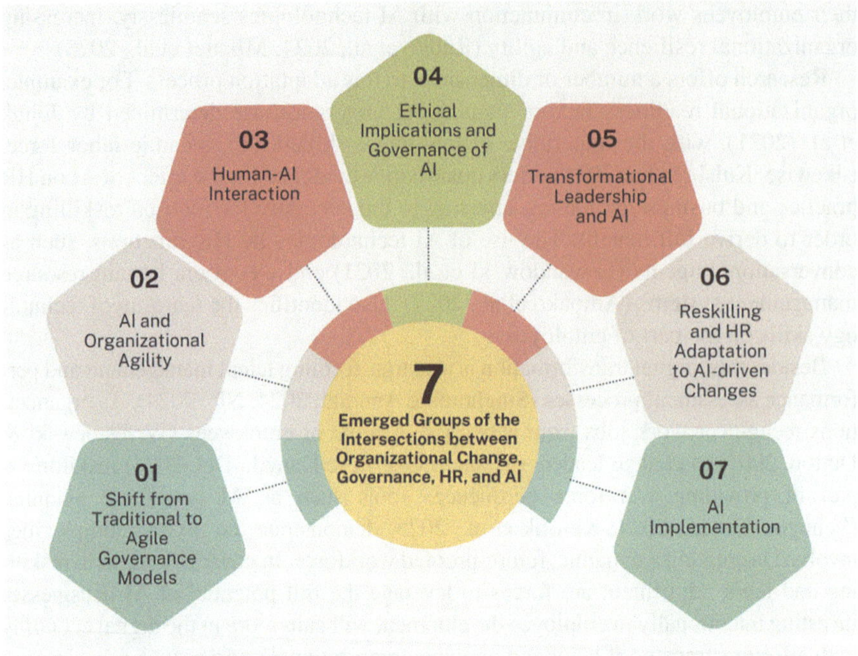

Fig. 5.5 Affinity diagram and seven emerged groups. (*Source: Author's creation*)

organizational performance, suggesting the integration of these practices will facilitate adoption.

Recent studies also examine deeper implications of AI implementation. Neumann et al. (2024) compare the deployment of AI in public agencies, with fundamental hindrances and enablers of success. Gendron et al. (2024) examine the social implications of AI, emphasizing the necessity of ethical and societal aspects at deployment. Lastly, organizational decision-making using AI is transforming paradigms of management, as projected by Shick et al. (2024), who affirm that AI has the ability to transform rationality in organizational decisions substantially.

Organizations can be capable of embracing AI adoption complexity through lessons from various industries and scholarly approaches to adopt AI sustainably and efficaciously (Fig. 5.5).

The systematic review, as per the affinity diagram, shows a definite inclination toward the adoption of AI in organizational governance models. It is not a technological innovation but an imperative shift of organizational structures and processes. The transition from traditional HR models to AI-based governance is toward more adaptive, responsive, and ethical organizational paradigms. The merging of the literature on new models of organizational governance for change management, specifically from the traditional HR models to the incorporation of AI integration, has made valuable contributions.

Emerging Organizational Models Reflect Governance in Change

6

Abstract

In this chapter, there is an elaborate examination of new organization models for leadership during a time of quick technological change, with the overarching focus being to shift from traditional HR models to AI-governance models. Using a literature systematic review and affinity mapping, seven unique yet interconnected themes are revealed to be AI-driven HR transformation, agility and adaptive models of governance, integration of digital technology, improved leadership models, evidence-based HR, cultural transformation, and ethical AI governance. Discussion also identifies the mechanisms through which the models enable responsiveness in the organization, encourage employees' engagement, and lead to innovation alongside tackling ethical and social issues. Practical tools like an AI Governance Decision Tree and implementation guidance are provided to assist organizations in attaining strategic adoption and overcoming organizational inertia and technological readiness issues.

In addressing the research question, *"What are the emerging organizational models for governing in change, focusing on transitioning from classical HR models to integrating artificial intelligence (AI)?"*

The below seven separate categories that came out of the SLR and the affinity method can be grouped under logical themes that are revealing of how new organizational designs shape governance in change that is responsive to shifting technological revolutions of AI (Fig. 6.1).

A. Rosa, *New Business Organizational Models for Governing in Times of Change*, Future of Business and Finance,
https://doi.org/10.1007/978-3-032-04091-6_6

Fig. 6.1 The seven emerging organizational models in the AI age (Source: SLR and affinity methods)

1. HR Transformation with AI and People-Centric Governance
   1.1 Career Development Through AI and AI-Driven Employee Experience
   1.2 Collaborative Leadership Models and Employee Satisfaction
2. Agility and Adaptability in Governance
   2.1 Flexible Governance Structures
   2.2 Holacratic Structures
   2.3 Flexibility and Innovation
3. Integration of Digital Technologies in Governance Structures
   3.1 AI-Optimized Organizational Performance
   3.2 Integration of AI in Governance Practices and Change Management Frameworks
4. AI-Enhanced Leadership Models and the Role of Transformational Leadership
5. Data-Driven-Informed HRM and Strategic Alignment of AI in HR
   5.1 AI-Powered Data-Driven Performance Management
6. AI-Based Cultural Transformation
7. Ethical AI-Based Governance

6.1 HR Transformation with AI and People-Centric Governance

6.1.1 Career Development Through AI and AI-Driven Employee Experience

In emerging organizational models to govern in change, organizations invest in continuous learning initiatives to prepare employees for new roles that require collaboration with AI technologies (Rudko et al., 2024; Mikalef et al., 2023). AI applications can enhance personalized learning and development.

AI promotes tailor-made training programs to individual employee needs, enhancing skill development and career progression (Khushk et al., 2025). AI streamlines HR processes and enhances employee interactions (Khushk et al., 2025). Integration of AI in workplace processes promotes HR's shared occupational identity (Bankins et al., 2024) and improves engagement and communication utilizing chatbots and virtual assistants (Gursoy & Cai, 2025).

Through virtual assistants and collaborative platforms, AI influences team dynamics and promotes new kinds of collaboration (Elkahlout et al., 2024). However, in order to promote cooperation and guarantee that AI enhances human expertise, roles and responsibilities must be redefined (Holmström & Carroll, 2024), and fair AI systems must be designed for employee management (Robert et al., 2020) and for HR performance evaluation (Nie, 2024).

On the other hand, the digital tools and employee experience management platforms reshape employee experiences in hybrid work (John et al., 2024).

A new application of job crafting theory to AI technology is provided by Perez et al. (2022), who take into account how the learning algorithms affect the workers' work experiences from their point of view. In response to AI adoption, employees' coordinated response across the three job crafting aspects including attempts to reposition their understanding of work, move toward more intimate relationships with clients, and rebalance their degrees of autonomy, which were first diminished by the arrival of AI, highlights how crucial these dimensions to together in order to successfully change employees' work experiences (Perez et al., 2022), which is demonstrates a shift toward dynamic and adaptive HR practices.

6.1.2 Collaborative Leadership Models and Employee Satisfaction

In the context of AI integration in HR, an organization's readiness for adopting and implementing AI is necessary (Jöhnk et al., 2021; Hradecky et al., 2022). Also, employee engagement and satisfaction to facilitate successful AI integration are increasingly mentioned as a priority in governance models (Divya et al., 2024), as well as understanding employee perceptions of AI pre-adoption in organizations (Chiu et al., 2021).

Divya et al. (2024) highlight that leadership influences AI success and employee engagement. Leadership is evolving in organizations by adopting AI (Ötting et al., 2021). Technological transformation and AI enhance employee engagement through collaborative leadership (Sarioguz & Miser, 2024). AI-supported leadership enhances employee engagement (Rožman et al., 2023; Divya et al., 2024) and is evolving toward collaborative approaches that engage employees in decision-making processes (Amoako et al., 2022).

6.2 Agility and Adaptability in Governance

In order for organizations to adapt quickly to changes in the business environment, the adoption of AI is encouraged (Rudko et al., 2024). AI represents a fast rate of innovation (Baumann & Wu, 2023), and agile organizational designs are required for implementation. Otherwise, AI implementation enables organizations to acquire the adaptability and agility required to drive change (Elkahlout et al., 2024) and direct innovation in a rapidly complex environment, which is an important development of organizational change management.

6.2.1 Flexible Governance Structures

The implementation of more flexible governance models allows organizations to respond more agilely and swiftly to market changes and challenges to adapt (Singhraul & Anuragi, 2024). and empowers organizational teams to make decisions and respond quickly to changes (Singhraul & Anuragi, 2024). In response to rapid technological changes, organizations need to design more adaptable governance models to foster innovation (Zheng, 2024) and adopt technological innovation. In a complex VUCA environment, the adoption of AI becomes a critical solution for improving process innovation (Gendron et al., 2024). AI can promote flatter organizational structures, enabling quicker and more decentralized decision-making (Gladden et al., 2022).

6.2.2 Holacratic Structures

The holacratic structures and the rise of decentralized management systems allow for enhancing dynamic roles and organizational responsiveness (Jatobá et al., 2023).

6.2.3 Adaptability, Flexibility, and Innovation

Building a culture that not only embraces change but also innovative thinking constitutes one of the organizational preparations for embracing AI (Olan et al., 2022; Jöhnk et al., 2021; Hradecky et al., 2022). Adoption of AI and encouraging AI innovation need an innovation culture that enables adaptive project management (Neumann et al., 2024), and employees are encouraged to experiment and learn from failure (Gendron et al., 2024). Organizational groups can explore machine learning and natural language processing, which have the ability to produce an innovation spasm (Papagiannidis et al., 2025).

6.3 Integration of Digital Technologies in Governance Structures

Emerging governance models in order to govern in change and adaptation in a turbulent environment need to embrace technological advancements. Expanding digital technology to new governance models provides communication and speeds up processes (Samir, 2024). Competitive markets and business trends press the use of AI (Maragno et al., 2023). Use of AI signifies a paradigm shift in organizational change. Flexibility and effectiveness are brought about through AI embedding, signifying a transformation of governance architecture toward adopting technological progress (Khushk et al., 2025). AI is currently recognized as a catalyst for identifying and driving strategic changes within organizations and is moving beyond its role as an innovative tool for efficiency (Khushk et al., 2025).

6.3.1 AI-Optimized Organizational Performance

The findings stress the dual benefit of AI in strategic planning and operational execution in organizations by streamlining processes, optimizing overall organizational performance, and, beyond that, enhancing decision-making capabilities. Practices in knowledge management and AI (Mahboub & Ghanem, 2024), including knowledge sharing (Olan et al., 2022), are enhancing the capacity to innovate and improve organizational performance.

Artificial intelligence tools can potentially give real-time performance information and feedback, allowing tailored employee development strategies and minimizing the time taken for performance reviews (Ali Mohamad et al., 2023).

6.3.2 Integration of AI in Governance Practices and Change Management Frameworks

Organizations, in order to enhance their change management processes, require embracing the strategies, including leaders' strong support, a supportive culture and structure, and advocating for the incorporation of cross-functional teams in change efforts (Piercy et al., 2013).

The integration of AI tools in established change management frameworks like Kotter's model can enhance an organization's ability to navigate complex transformations (Nie, 2024), representing a critical advancement in governance in change.

AI tools, by evaluating enormous data in real time, enhance leaders' insights to guide strategic changes (Shrestha et al., 2019).

6.4 AI-Enhanced Leadership Models and the Role of Transformational Leadership

The concept of governance in change, which characterizes the transition from a dynamic environment to a turbulent environment, requires leaders who lead organizations in a turbulent environment.

AI-mediated leadership models present leaders with data-driven insights that enhance decision-making processes (Nie, 2024), empower leaders to develop a more accurate understanding of the challenges and opportunities created by change, and support informed and timely change initiatives to adapt to change, also enhancing leadership capabilities and providing insights into performance and team dynamics (Nie, 2024).

However, resistance to change as a pervasive theme in literature, especially psychological and cultural resistance to change (Tambe et al., 2019), will likely hinder the take-up of emerging technologies such as AI.

Organizations that are pursuing a transformational leadership style and leaders who inspire and motivate their teams to embrace change can drive effective change (Mouazen et al., 2024). Transformational leadership can transform an innovative culture and guide an organization toward embracing new technology. Moreover, it is necessary to commit to powerful leadership and communication clarity regarding the reasons behind change and transformation necessity to reduce resistance and develop a shared purpose and effective integration of AI (Zheng, 2024). Recognition and integration of informal networks and social network analysis (SNA) that provides insights into power structures that may not be immediately visible through traditional hierarchical models, in organizational change efforts, reflect a shift toward more flexible governance models, and also enhance knowledge sharing and informing governance strategies (Bonanomi et al., 2020).

6.5 Driven Data-Informed HRM and Strategic Alignment of AI in HR

The findings regarding emerging organizational models for governing in change highlight a significant shift from traditional human resource (HR) approaches to more innovative, data-driven methodologies. The shift from intuition-based HR to analytical, data-driven practices reflects a growing adoption of AI analytics in HR (Venugopal et al., 2024).

For Industry 4.0, the adoption of AI in HR is essential (Smith et al., 2024) if organizations are to prosper in the current technological environment. In terms of data-driven HRM, AI-based data insights in HR management contribute to creating value in the case of strategic alignment of AI in HR (Venugopal et al., 2024). Also,

AI-based real-time data analytics contribute to supporting informed HR decisions and evaluating HR performance (Samir, 2024). AI-powered HR systems automate routine decisions, therefore enabling leaders to focus on strategic issues (Elkahlout et al., 2024).

In terms of HR, AI automates tasks, freeing up HR to concentrate on more strategic projects (Benbya et al., 2020). AI tools, in order to be successful in implementation, need to be in line with business goals and HRM as a whole. To guarantee that AI initiatives and HR policies, and practices support the broader strategic objectives of the organization, the strategic alignment that facilitates a cohesive approach to transformation is necessary (Khushk et al., 2025). Aligning AI initiatives with organizational goals enhances the strategic function of HR (Khushk et al., 2025).

6.5.1 AI-Powered Data-Driven Performance Management

The move toward data-driven performance management and the incorporation of AI analysis marks a transformative phase in organizational leadership in performance management, representing a pivotal change in how organizations assess the effectiveness of their change initiatives in governing in change practices. AI has the potential to revolutionize management practices and make them more productive and efficient.

AI is superior to humans in data processing and pattern recognition (Benbya et al., 2020). By utilizing concrete data, organizations are enabled to make informed adjustments in real time.

This technology-driven method improves not only performance measurement reliability but also maximizes change communication, making it efficient and engaging. Furthermore, AI assists companies to monitor both internal as well as external trends, and this leads to anticipatory decision-making (Atanassova et al., 2025).

Artificial intelligence is transforming performance management systems by leveraging data analysis in a bid to customize development programs, detect skills gaps, and provide personalized feedback (Mikalef et al., 2023) thereby data-driven performance management facilitates a culture of accountability and transparency because teams can monitor progress toward certain metrics and outcomes.

6.6 AI-Supported Cultural Transformation, Integration, and Collaboration

For effective governance in change, it is necessary to take cultural dynamics into account to show how culture affects the success of AI integration. A supportive culture is necessary to meet the need to challenge the status quo and address resistance to change (Piercy et al., 2013).

Emphasis on steady growth and a culture of constant learning and adjustment is important to enable change (Venugopal et al., 2024). Through steady growth, organizations can ensure their HR holds the required skills and knowledge to participate in change processes. Building a holistic culture that supports collaboration among teams is essential for successful change management (Zheng, 2024).

Organizations can effectively manage change by promoting an experimentation culture; teams can investigate AI applications and gain knowledge from mistakes by promoting an experimental mindset.

Apart from that, by engaging the staff in the transition process through open communication, alleviation workers' anxiety about job displacement, and facilitating reskilling and upskilling, organizations can respond to changing practices successfully. Companies with proper utilization of AI technologies can establish a more flexible work environment where the employees are not only receptive to changes but also seek them out; they are encouraged to try and experiment, thereby leading to a more flexible organizational culture.

6.7 Ethical and Responsible AI Governance

The research on emerging organizational models of change indicates a general trend toward embracing ethical, accountable, and sustainable practices in change management, notably in the context of adopting AI. As per Fatmawati et al. (2024), change management in good governance models is formulated with ethical values. With organizations becoming increasingly dependent on AI technology to cause change in fluid environments, there is a requirement to bring in elements of fairness, responsibility, and inclusivity into change and develop frameworks for their implementation (Nie, 2024). Emphasis on steady growth and a culture of constant learning and adjustment is important to enable change (Venugopal et al., 2024).

Through steady growth, organizations can ensure their HR holds the required skills and knowledge to participate in change processes. Building a holistic culture that supports collaboration among teams is essential for successful change management (Zheng, 2024).

Organizations are able to leverage AI to assist them in monitoring compliance with ethical practices and sustainability goals (Jatobá et al., 2023). Also, incorporating sustainability practices in governance models alongside ethical practices (Jatobá et al., 2023) and aligning with Sustainable Development Goals, in an era where environmental and social responsibilities are increasingly scrutinized, is required for organizations to govern in change. By implementing sustainability regulatory frameworks, organizations can enhance their reputation, attract talent, and ensure compliance with evolving.

The research findings indicate that the shift to AI-based HR models offers firms an efficient model of leadership during times of change. The results call on organizations to adopt these new governance models proactively, recognizing that effective management of the digital shift demands innovative HR practices attuned to the changing business environment. The new organizational models for governance of change management in general mark a dramatic departure from traditional HR paradigms toward more integrated, collaborative, and adaptive ones. These emerging models signal a huge organizational governance model shift, with the emphasis on the transition from traditional HR practices to more adaptive, HR-focused, and data-driven models. The convergence of AI and digital technologies is at the forefront of this shift, which requires a fixation on ethical matters, cultural transformation, and cooperative leadership to handle change complexities in an effective manner.

The results of the systematic review show a clear trend toward the incorporation of AI in organizational models of governance toward more adaptive and responsive models. The transcendence of traditional HR models to AI-facilitated governance is a paradigm shift in organizational functioning. The study provides evidence that now organizations are inclined toward models emphasizing responsiveness and agility over rigidity and control. This transformation is enabled by AI technologies, which give organizations the ability to operate in a complicated world.

The seven unique dimensions identified in this study, AI-driven HR transformation and employee-centric governance, agility and adaptability in governance, incorporation of digital technologies in governance structures, AI-augmented leadership models and the function of transformational leadership, data-informed HRM and the strategic Alignment of AI in HR, AI-supported cultural transformation, integration and collaboration, and ethical and responsible AI governance together paint a comprehensive picture of a seismic change that organizations embrace in governance in a time of relentless disruption.

These new models drift from a rigid, top-down organization and reactive HR practices to fluid, adaptive, and proactive ones, enabled by AI and digital technologies.

"A focus on employee-driven governance, with AI-driven personalized development and enriched experiences, highlights a realization that engaged and skilled employees are necessary to navigate change." The adoption of agile and decentralized governance such as holacratic systems, for instance, points to the desire for organizations to become more fleet-footed and to adapt quickly to volatile market conditions. Deep and Complete Digital and AI integration: It will not only streamline business operations but will also offer insights to leaders to influence strategic change programs like never before! Progressing leadership models toward more collaborative and transformational types is critical to creating a culture that thrives on change and innovation.

In addition, the importance given to evidence-based HRM and the strategic embedding of AI with HR practices expressed in this monograph attest to evidence-based decision-making in managing human capital in times of disruptions. This emphasis on AI-enabled culture change also highlights the critical importance of generating a culture in which staff are primed not to simply accept change but to design it. Lastly, the imperative focus of ethical and responsible AI governance further illustrates an increasing appreciation of the implications for society of technology's stride into the business world and a sense that businesses do better when they act with fairness and transparency and are held to account.

6.7.1 The Adaptation Decision Tree and AI Governance Guide

To empower managers to effectively implement and adapt the above proposed governance models, this section offers practical tools, including a decision tree and guiding principles that facilitate contextual customization and strategic decision-making. Providing these frameworks in the monograph will promote its practical contribution and help managers to adopt the novel emerging organizational models assuredly through diverse organizational environments.

6.7.1.1 The AI Governance Guide (Fig. 6.2)

The Adaptation Decision Tree

In this section, we offer a transferable framework, adopting a Decision Tree (ADT) for AI-enabled governance. The (ADT) is a graphical step-by-step diagram that streamlines complicated decision-making procedures, can be applied across different industries, sizes, and cultures, and provides clear steps and checkpoints. ADT intended to assist managers in assessing their organizational readiness and identifying the correct governance model in terms of AI integration and change management. The ADT aids managers to systematically weigh internal and external factors in choosing, adapting, and implementing suitable governance models for their organization (Fig. 6.3).

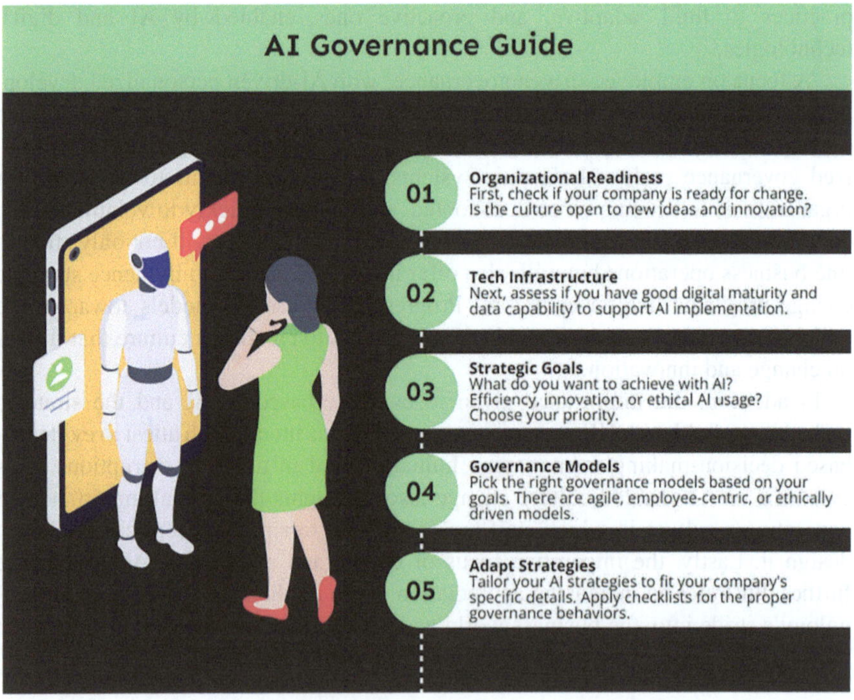

Fig. 6.2 AI governance guide for organizations

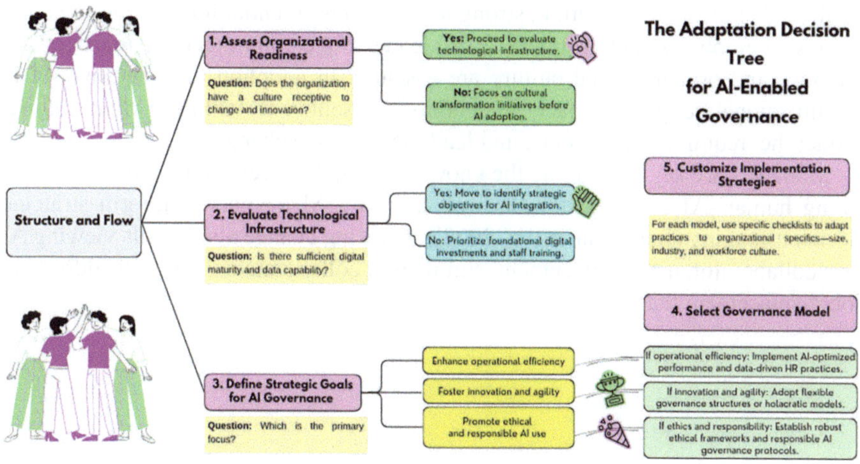

Fig. 6.3 Adopting a decision tree for AI-enabled governance

6.7.2 AI Governance Implementation: Overcoming Obstacles and Organizational Inertia

Mimetic pressures lead firms to emulate successful adopters in order to preclude obsolescence (Agrawal, 2024). Institutional pressures, such as coercive and mimetic, also drive adoption. Industry norms are driving organizations to implement AI solutions.

The diffusion of innovation theory also provides some considerations, noting that perceived relative advantage, compatibility, trialability, complexity, and observability are factors that have a significant effect on the adoption process (Agrawal, 2024).

However, the successful implementation of AI-based governance is confronted with substantial real-world challenges that have their basis in organizational dynamics as well as the complexities inherent to AI.

One of the biggest challenges is bridging the "readiness gap" between workers and the organization, which requires extensive awareness and upskilling initiatives (Ooi et al., 2023). This human factor is compounded by possible resistance arising due to fears over data security, privacy, algorithmic bias, and perceived removal of humans from decision-making.

The demand for transparent and understandable AI choices, along with general ethical aspects, is very important for mass adoption (Ooi et al., 2023).

Apart from individual and ethical matters, organizational inertia can be considered as significant of an obstacle. Successful AI deployment requires rethinking existing arrangements at the very base level, needing solid technology foundations and infrastructure investments (Sandkuhl, 2019). Usually, it requires overcoming different organizational, technological, and environmental obstacles, recognized by models such as the Technology–Organization–Environment (TOE) paradigm (Misra et al., 2023). In such a situation, strong leadership is essential for overcoming challenges, as emphasized by Agrawal (2024) leadership commitment, top management support, and organizational culture are essential in adoption of generative AI in organizational settings. In fact, leadership is essential to build the right culture, attract the required investments, and lead the initiative change.

Managers are key to bridging the knowledge gap between humans and AI, facilitating human–AI collaboration, as well as using AI insights to inform strategic decision-making (Baumann & Wu, 2023). Resisting change also entails viewing AI as a collaborator, not a replacement, stimulating collaborative work, and addressing job displacement fear.

What Are the Distinctions Between Governing in Change and Governing Change?

7

Abstract

This chapter examines the changing landscape of complex governance in the midst of unstable and murky environments, with the utmost difference between "governing change" and "governing in change." This chapter provokes an anticipatory, ethics-led approach to governance that values agility, personnel engagement, and responsible utilization of AI so that organizations can adapt and succeed in the turbulence of modern change. In essence, it inspires a new-fashioned approach to governance—that is, governance in and through change as opposed to managing change—guarantees organizational resilience and competitiveness in a progressively changing global environment.

Similar to navigating a ship through choppy seas, in the complexity of contemporary governance situations, leaders, in order to preserve stability in the face of ongoing changing circumstances, need to be adaptable quickly to unanticipated developments, which means "governing in change." While leaders in "governing in change" try to maintain their flexibility to quickly adjust policies and tactics, "governing change" refers to controlling change proactively.

7.1 Transitioning from Dynamic to Turbulent Environments

For management, the transition from an active to a chaotic environment is an opportunity and a challenge. Through the establishment of a culture of continuous learning and development, companies can be able to sustain their agility while

A. Rosa, *New Business Organizational Models for Governing in Times of Change*, Future of Business and Finance,
https://doi.org/10.1007/978-3-032-04091-6_7

experimenting with new things and learning new approaches and businesses while still sustaining their fundamental objectives and values.

Within today's modern scene marked by VUCA environment, organizations confront uncommon challenges that require a re-evaluation of conventional administration systems.

We argue that the distinction between "governing in change" and "governing change" is particularly significant as organizations explore transitioning from Dynamic to turbulent environments and experience new complexities introduced by AI and digital innovations. These innovative technologies speed change and create additional challenges, necessitating organizations to be more adaptable. Hence, "Governing in Change" becomes essential, since it supplies the foundational mindset and structures needed for organizations to combat the transition from dynamic to turbulent environments raised by digital transformation effectively. "Governing in Change" ensures organizations can flourish amidst chaos, promoting innovation while managing related risks.

7.2 The Importance of Adjustment and Governing in Change

The concept of "governing in change" represents the ability to lead and flexibility amidst chaotic circumstances. As Miao and Nduneseokwu (2024) express, the complexities of the twenty-first-century trade environment are beyond the grasp of conventional administration speculations established in steadiness and control.

These routine standards, regularly characterized by bureaucratic structures and Taylorism, are progressively lacking for organizations confronting fast and erratic shifts. Instead, the requirement for flexible leadership—leaders who can viably explore and react to rising challenges is basic.

In a world where incremental headways are insufficient to address the multifaceted challenges posed by a VUCA environment, organizations must make organizational frameworks that prioritize agility, flexibility, and nonstop learning. As Atanassova et al. (2025) emphasize, effective authority in this setting requires an attitude that sees change as a consistent, developing a culture of inventiveness and adaptability. The rise of AI innovations assists in complicating this scene, as organizations must coordinate these innovations into their frameworks while remaining sensitive to moral considerations and a human-centric view.

7.3 The Transition from Governing Change to Governing in Change

Whereas "Governing Change" infers a focus on overseeing particular change activities, "Governing in Change" speaks to a more all-encompassing approach that coordinates change as a crucial aspect of organizational elements. As organizations go up against disturbances stemming from worldwide supply chains and innovative progressions, the capacity to "administer within the storm" gets to be basic. This viewpoint emphasizes the requirement for leaders to develop situations that energize development, flexibility, and collaboration, encouraging a proactive reaction to outside pressures.

Newly rising organizational models reflect this move toward "Governing in Change." These models prioritize employee-centric administration, deftness, and the integration of computerized innovations, including AI. For instance, organizations are progressively embracing collaborative administration models that improve HR engagement and satisfaction, as highlighted by Divya et al. (2024). AI-driven experiences can encourage this engagement, enabling leaders to make well-informed choices that align with HR needs and desires.

7.4 The Role of AI in Governing in Change

AI isn't simply a means for improving operational proficiency; it means an essential change in organizational administration. As Joseph and Sengul (2025) contend, organizations must deliberately comprehend and use AI's potential to explore the complexities of the present-day UVCA environment. This integration requires a move from simply managing change to proactively governing within it, emphasizing the significance of moral AI hone and human–AI collaboration. In terms of the role of AI in governing in change, it allows organizations to foster continuous advancement by leveraging artificial intelligence to inform decisions based on data, monitor progress, and identify areas for improvement (Venugopal et al., 2024).

In fact, the incorporation of AI into governance structures not only improves the efficacy of change activities but also allows organizations to embrace more adaptable systems that improve responsiveness to change to explore the complexities of a rapidly evolving environment.

7.5 Ethical Considerations in Governing in Change

The moral consequences of AI selection cannot be ignored. As organizations progressively depend on AI advances, they must prioritize moral administration practices that advance fairness, responsibility, and inclusivity. This includes tending to concerns related to algorithmic prejudice, information protection, and the potential disintegration of human aptitudes.

By building up systems that administer the moral utilization of AI, organizations can construct trust with HR and other stakeholders, improving their flexibility and flexibility in times of transformation.

In summary, the differentiation between "Governing Change" and "Governing in Change" underscores the requirement for organizations to advance their administration systems in response to the complexities of the advanced commerce environment. "Governing in Change," characterized by flexible leadership, employee-centric models, and moral AI integration, is essential for organizations to flourish in a VUCA world.

Conclusion and Final Thoughts 8

Abstract

This chapter summarizes the monograph and calls for organizational governance to evolve in the presence of a VUCA scenario. It calls for a shift in the paradigm of classical HR models to futuristic, AI-driven models that facilitate greater agility, strategic choice, and stakeholder engagement. Theory contributions are expanding theory to the use of AI in change management, adapting industry-specific solutions, and incorporating ethical frameworks in AI implementation. Managerial and policy implications underscore the need for creating AI-ready cultures, strategic alignment, and accountable AI governance as ways of remaining competitive and viable. Limitations and possible paths for further research are delineated, with a focus on the value of longitudinal, empirical studies across numerous settings in establishing a deeper understanding of the power of AI to transform.

The critical evolution of organizational governance and embracing new organizational models to navigate the turbulent changing environment in response to a VUCA environment has been examined in this monograph, "New Business Organizational Models for Governing in Times of Change: From Classical HR Models to the Role of AI." Effective governance under a turbulent changing environment, according to the main thesis, requires the capacity to maneuver through uncertain settings by effectively controlling "structural determinants," especially the dynamic interactions between individuals, organizations, and outside factors. With artificial intelligence (AI) emerging as a key factor, this paradigm change from

A. Rosa, *New Business Organizational Models for Governing in Times of Change*, Future of Business and Finance,
https://doi.org/10.1007/978-3-032-04091-6_8

a dynamic but predictable environment to one that is rapid and unpredictable necessitates a fundamental reevaluation of classical HR models and the embrace of innovative models. The research findings, which may be divided into seven main themes, offer important insights into how new organizational models represent governance in transition and keep up with artificial intelligence's quick technological breakthroughs.

In the present volatile and dynamic world, it is imperative to incorporate AI into governance. This monograph, suggesting an active and human-centric approach to sailing through the turbulent waters of change with new organizational designs, delved into the shift from traditional HR to AI-driven organizational models, highlighting the use of AI in change management. The research conclusions of this monograph include the trend toward AI-based leadership, embracing a novel shift, which necessitates engaging in an HR-centric way that combines technology with ethics, and propose that organizations implement AI and frame AI strategies for HR reskilling in an attempt to boost efficiency, innovation, and sustainability.

This monograph has discussed the required transformation of organizational governance in an increasingly turbulent world environment. The broad hypothesis is that effective governance of complexity requires the capacity to navigate uncertain contexts through strategic management of "structural determinants" and specifically, dynamic interdependence among people, organizations, and externalities. This paradigm change from a dynamic but deterministic to a rapid and uncertain world requires an entire re-conceptualization of conventional human resource (HR) models and the adoption of new paradigms, with artificial intelligence (AI) being a primary driving force.

The findings of the research, grouped into seven different themes, offer an insightful understanding of how new organizational models are a reflection of governance in transformation, in accordance with the speedy technological changes of AI.

The seven emerging organizational models for governing in change, focusing on transitioning from classical HR models to integrating artificial intelligence (AI) identified through the systematic literature review and affinity method, reflect governance in change that aligns with the rapid technological advancements of AI. The emerging organizational models demonstrate a basic shift from transactional HR practices to transformational HR practices, driven by AI's capacity to automate routine tasks and enable a focus on strategic employee development and experience. The emerging organizational models benefit from AI to inform strategic HR decisions, guide change and empower employees, facilitate quick adaptation against shifting environments through agile organizational structures, evolve leadership toward more collaborative systems, and improve organizational performance. "They promote collaboration, continuous learning, and a willingness to experiment with new technologies by focusing on cultivating an AI-ready organizational culture."

8.1 Theoretical Implications

From a theoretical perspective, this review consolidates current research findings, highlighting the influential dimensions and benefits of AI. It establishes a structured understanding of the technology within the context of the organization and HR. Overall, the intersection of the Or-AI nexus and emerging patterns in the examined topics emphasizes the multidimensional impact of AI on organizations.

The findings provide an exhaustive cartography of novel organizational designs plugging the research gaps identified in the introduction. The sets of findings each contribute toward filling each of the research challenges, building up knowledge on the effective implementation of change governance using AI in modern-day organizations. From the ensuing discourse, the illustration of how the sets of studies fill and attend to the introduced gaps is understood.

The research results of this monograph contribute to previous literature in six distinct aspects, outlining the theoretical implications of this work.

It is crucial to explore how AI is fundamentally reshaping HR processes. As indicated by Jatobá et al. (2023), there is a significant research gap in establishing how AI has a direct connection to change management procedures and governance structures. Therefore, the first theoretical contribution of this monograph is to fill this research gap and understand the connection between AI and change management procedures. The research findings demonstrate that this is achieved through detailed mechanisms of AI in performance, HR, and strategic processes. The monograph's research findings show how AI can act as a transformative tool in governing change by supporting innovative particular processes, including improving personalized learning (Khushk et al., 2025), promoting communication through chatbots (Gursoy & Cai, 2025), effectively changing experiences of employees in the workplace and enhancing adaptive human resource systems (Perez et al., 2022), utilizing real-time data (Samir, 2024), and performance analytics based on AI (Olan et al., 2022).

The above findings provide specific insights into AI's contribution to facilitating change management. Furthermore, the organizational performance that is optimized by AI (Ali Mohamad et al., 2023) and the implementation of AI in the governance process are promoting understanding of the way AI improves operational agility and strategic planning.

The second theoretical contribution of this study can be summarized as follows. The research addresses the gap in research in the lack of industry-designed and contextualized models (Jatobá et al., 2023). According to Jatobá et al. (2023), literature tends to deliver generalized results with little or no consideration of industry-designed problems and solutions, and thus the necessity for customized organizational models and governance approaches.

With regard to the "Collaborative Leadership Models," findings indicate that technological transformation and AI enhance employee engagement through collaborative leadership (Sarioguz & Miser, 2024; Rožman et al., 2023; Divya et al., 2024) and engage employees in decision-making processes (Amoako et al., 2022).

In terms of "Agility and Adaptability," in organizations, due to AI having a rapid pace of innovation, agile organizational structures are necessary for its adoption (Baumann & Wu, 2023), and to adapt quickly to changes in the business environment, the adoption of AI is encouraged for organizations (Rudko et al., 2024). At the same time, embracing AI helps organizations to gain the agility and adaptability required to govern in change (Elkahlout et al., 2024).

With regard to the "Cultural Transformation," new governance models highlight cultivating a supportive culture to facilitate the adoption of change (Zheng, 2024) and the necessity of an AI-friendly culture, which is necessary to embrace innovation and change to maximize the benefits of AI integration (Rožman et al., 2023). Thus, organizational culture emphasis, stakeholder involvement, and ethics principles further contextualize such models to individual organizational settings.

By offering sophisticated models that include organizational culture, leadership, and ethical factors, these findings address the gap in terms of the lack of industry-specific and contextualized models. They show that change governance is not a one-size-fits-all process but a modified, flexible model that is sensitive to organizational culture and industry demands.

The third theoretical contribution of this study addresses filling the research gap mentioned by Jatobá et al. (2023), who argue that the dynamics of human–AI collaboration within new governance models remain underexplored; in fact, there is a lack of understanding regarding how HR and AI systems can effectively synergize. Studies on "AI-Driven Career Development" openly address human–AI interaction, stressing the necessity to redefine work, encourage collaboration, and involve employees in change efforts.

The monograph findings in terms of "AI-Driven Career Development" detail how, in emerging organizational models to govern in change, AI can facilitate career advancement by customizing training programs to each employee's needs (Khushk et al., 2025). And also, the research findings augment that organizations' investment in continuous learning initiatives prepares employees for new roles that require collaboration with AI technologies (Rudko et al., 2024; Mikalef et al., 2023).

Hence, these findings bridge the gap as far as the narrow insight concerning human–AI collaboration and employee attitudes are concerned by presenting specific illustrations of how organizations can design roles, develop trust, and create a culture to embrace AI.

The fourth theoretical contribution of this monograph is in connection with filling the gap regarding how AI can transform human-centered design (HCD) principles and strategic HR partnerships. In relation to this gap, the current study results illustrated personalized HR practices and alignment strategies that incorporate AI thoughtfully. AI can enable personalized employee development plans, offer continuous feedback, and performance analytics (Ali Mohamad et al., 2023).

The discussion of "AI-driven HR Transformation" and "Data-Informed HRM" illustrates how AI can be integrated with human-oriented practices, such as job crafting (Perez et al., 2022; Raisch & Fomina, 2023), AI-enabled HR analytics in the context of job crafting (Bagis & Yulianeu, 2024), and AI crafting (Li et al., 2024) that presents leader AI crafting is positively related to employee AI crafting and to employee AI engagement (Li et al., 2024).

In addition, the focus on strategic alignment of AI initiatives with HR policies (Hradecky et al., 2022) highlights the need to integrate AI in a thoughtful manner within larger HR contexts. In fact, human judgment is still essential for coming to strategic decisions, even when AI can automate data processing and analysis (Azzam & Beckmann, 2022). These findings aid in addressing the gap between how AI can revolutionize human-centered design (HCD) principles and strategic HR partnerships by offering models that stress individualization, collaboration, and strategic emphasis, facilitating more successful HR redesign practices.

As the fifth theoretical contribution of this monograph, this research addressed the need for frameworks for ethical, responsible, and sustainable AI governance. As mentioned by Divya et al. (2024), more investigation is urgently needed on the ethical and social implications of AI in HR and governance. Also, according to Singhraul and Anuragi (2024), the challenges, such as the ethical use of AI and data privacy concerns, are inadequately covered in the literature.

The monograph's research findings show that designing frameworks to increase stakeholder engagement, fairness, transparency, and accountability can address these gaps in the literature. Research findings advocate for embedding ethical principles into AI deployment and proposing governance models rooted in responsibility supports long-term social acceptance and sustainability.

As mentioned by Agrawal (2024), creating rules and regulations for the ethical and responsible application of AI is part of this. According to Nie (2024), in change initiatives, including inclusivity, accountability, and fairness, is significant as well as when implementing AI, including transparency and bias in decision-making (Papagiannidis et al., 2025).

As for the sixth theoretical contribution, the study addresses the scarcity of longitudinal and empirical studies on AI's impacts on Intelligent human resources highlighted by Jatobá et al. (2023). Although the study outcomes are mostly about conceptual models, longitudinal empirical evidence is scarce; they bridge the gap halfway by highlighting the necessity of ongoing adaptation, learning cultures, and performance monitoring necessary for long-term sustainability.

8.2 Implications for Policy-Makers

8.2.1 Promoting AI Adoption Through Policy Support

Government authorities have to promote the take-up of AI technologies by companies through increased accessibility of financial aid, such as grants, tax credits, and subsidies. This will make it easier to transition toward AI-based government systems that offer transparency to competition and innovation in the market.

8.2.2 Investing in Ecosystems of Data and Infrastructure

Policymakers, in order to support organizations to implement AI effectively for operational and strategic goals, by invest in the development of shared digital platforms, enabling access to integrated data stores to lower transaction costs, and promote ecosystems of Data and infrastructure to improve decision-making based on data.

8.2.3 Promoting Industry-Specific and Contextualized AI Strategies

Identifying the special challenges and potentials of various industries by advocating for adapted AI governance schemes. Encouraging pilot schemes and studies under individual sectors can facilitate evolving best practices applicable to specific organizational environments, thereby facilitating better AI integration.

8.2.4 Encouraging Long-Term and Empirical Research

Encouraging empirical studies and conducting longitudinal examination on the implications of the implementation of AI in organizations and their influence on governance, social outcomes, and HR well-being. This proof can be employed to inform policymakers of ongoing improvement in governance systems.

8.2.5 Enabling Cross-Sector Collaboration and Knowledge Sharing

Regarding the major responsibility of policymakers to design and establishing an suitable ecosystem that promotes AI-based organizational governance, with respect to the ethical principles, policymakers through instituting policies to support making arenas for dialogue among government agencies, industry leaders, scholars, and civil society to exchange information and co-design an ecosystem to tackle issues in the VUCA environment, can enhance the public value of AI technologies, and maximize the potential of AI for socio-economic gains.

This study adds to theoretical knowledge on organizational change management and governance in a number of significant ways. It initially adds to existing theory by pointing out the inadequacies of traditional HR models in addressing the complexity of an uncertain operating environment.

The research underscores the need for paradigm shifts toward adaptive, agile, and technology-savvy governance systems. Second, it offers a new perspective on the AI role, not only as an automation and efficiency aid, but also as a central driver changing organizational design, leadership, and HR. The generated themes, i.e., AI-driven HR transformation, agile governance, and AI-enabled leadership, offer a richer theoretical basis for the research of the impact of AI on organizational dynamics. In addition, placing emphasis on the ethical and moral application of AI adds to the body of knowledge on how AI affects society, in this case, within the organizational context. This study also offers a conceptual framework on the intersection of technological innovation and established organizational theory, such as job crafting, transformational leadership, and change management models, and demonstrates that these can be improved and reconfigured through the use of AI.

8.3 Managerial Implications

The results are highly relevant from a managerial viewpoint. In particular, they demonstrate that organizations have much to gain by adopting AI in different operational areas. With AI, an organization can increase competitiveness, enhance customer satisfaction, authenticate products, and streamline essential processes. Secondly, this monograph highlights the emerging trends and adoption of AI-based models in organizations and provides insights to organizations to improve performance and enhance competitive advantage by developing and implementing AI-based innovation in their organizational sectors.

The results underline the necessity of preemptive AI adoption by organizations as a core governance initiative, rather than an additive technology. There should be the creation of an "AI-ready" organizational culture that respects ongoing learning, flexibility, and innovation. The study emphasizes moving toward employee-centric governance models in which AI is utilized to optimize employee experience, tailor development, and enhance collaboration. In addition, the study emphasizes the changing role of leadership, with the importance of transformational and collaborative leadership that can lead organizations through AI deployment and cultural transformation successfully.

8.4 Implications for Practice

Understanding what drives technology innovation, including the innovation of early adopters, helps organizations make better AI implementation decisions. Understanding these drivers, organizations are able to optimize the use of new technologies, create innovation, and achieve competitiveness in volatile and dynamic markets. The applied importance of this research is multifaceted. HR practitioners are urged to transcend their role as mere traditional administrative managers and utilize data analysis and AI technology for strategic HR decision-making. Adoption of AI-powered platforms for talent attraction, performance management, and employee development and growth, for instance, as this research recommends, equates to more effective and tailored HR practices. Organizations need to focus on developing flexible, holacratic organizations that motivate teams and enable change readiness at speed. The convergence of digital technology with governance frameworks is no longer a choice but an imperative to enable better communication, automate, and streamline organizational performance.

8.5 Limitations and Future Directions

The main limitation of this study lies in the fact that it is a selective review of a relatively restricted number of papers. This relative lack of research is because AI's integration into HR and organizations is still in its infancy. However, by contributing to the knowledge of the field's understanding of AI adoption in an innovative way, this comprehensive literature review contributes to the current body of knowledge. Empirical studies, case studies, and quantitative studies can possibly expand and validate these results in future research. Longitudinal studies can possibly demonstrate the long-term consequences of AI adoption on business performance and corporate governance. Comparative studies are also necessary across various industries and organizational contexts (public sector, SMEs).

Case Studies on AI Solutions in HR and Monograph Insights

9

Abstract

This chapter depicts the transformative effect of artificial intelligence (AI) on human resource management (HRM) by way of a series of comprehensive case studies and monograph research findings. It depicts how AI technologies such as natural language processing, machine learning, and predictive analytics are reshaping HR activities by making them efficient, fair, and decision-making focused. Case points like HireVue, LinkedIn Recruiter, Talla, IBM Watson Talent, etc., have applications that range from automated candidate sorting to personalized employee development to predictive turnover estimation and diversity reporting.

Throughout the series of in-depth case studies and monograph insights, we seek to investigate the transformative potential of artificial intelligence (AI) in the personnel and human resource management (HRM) domain. As AI, in the form of natural language processing and machine learning, and predictive analytics, becomes a staple in the daily operations of an organization, it is also beginning to transform traditional HR processes by accelerating efficiency, objectivity, and strategic thought. In this chapter, we discuss how front-runners in solutions are exceeding it, from automated candidate assessment with HireVue to personalized employee development from Docebo. In addition, this chapter covers and references critical topics, including AI-enabled organizational models, agile governance, digital integration, leadership evolution, and ethics, and provides examples of how AI can enable a more open, distributed, and fact-based HR future. In these case studies, we want to ensure that readers can see the big picture of how AI is helping to not only

A. Rosa, *New Business Organizational Models for Governing in Times of Change*, Future of Business and Finance,
https://doi.org/10.1007/978-3-032-04091-6_9

enhance HR functions but also to serve as a catalyst for wider organizational change that is in keeping with modern governance and cultural demands.

9.1 Case Studies on AI Solutions in HR

9.1.1 HireVue

Uses NLP and machine learning to automate resume screening and candidate matching, supporting better shortlisting quality with less bias.

HireVue uses sophisticated Natural Language Processing (NLP) and supervised machine learning methods to pre-screen the first phase of candidate evaluation. In particular, its NLP algorithms are taught on gargantuan resumes and job descriptions databases to extract and match textual features that identify keywords, phrases, and semantic profiles that point to suitable skills, experience, and qualifications. At the same time, algorithm-based machine classifiers like support vector machines (SVMs) or deep neural networks are trained on past hiring data to make forecasts about candidate fit and aptness. The aim is to subdue human cognition biases (e.g., confirmation bias and halo effect) that unconsciously affect conventional resume screening, thus increasing inter-rater reliability and fostering an unbiased shortlisting process. This strategy is congruent with regulating algorithmic decision-making, underscoring greater choice and less undesired impact in terms of employment through data-driven candidate matching.

9.1.2 LinkedIn Recruiter

Identifies candidates with the right skills and experience to achieve hiring faster and maximize hiring effectiveness. LinkedIn Recruiter uses advanced AI algorithms such as graph neural networks and collaborative filtering algorithms to optimize candidate sourcing and identification. Its AI algorithms process a rich set of data, including user profiles, skill endorsements, work history, educational history, and professional networks. From these data points, the platform can infer latent candidate features and infer the likelihood that a candidate has the necessary skills and experience for a given job. The machine learning algorithms driving the system are upgraded constantly through recruiter feedback from interactions and hiring decisions in order to maximize recall and accuracy. This enables a quicker and more focused talent acquisition with lower time-to-hire and quality of hire through predictive identification of suitable candidates from a large professional network.

9.1.3 Talla

Provides an AI assistant for onboarding, answering questions, and delivering training material, enhancing onboarding speed.

Talla is an NLP-enabled chatbot with rule-based support for intent and entity extraction. It is mainly used to automate the induction process by giving immediate and correct responses to frequently asked questions by new recruits about company assets, procedures, and policies. Through automated information provision and demand-based delivery of learning content, Talla hopes to eliminate administrative work for HR personnel and speed up new-hire assimilation into company culture. This product represents the idea of intelligent automation and self-service HR to facilitate a more improved new-hire experience and perhaps decrease human HR representative cognitive workload.

9.1.4 IBM Watson Talent

Uses performance data for unbiased ratings and discovers areas for people to be trained. IBM Watson Talent applies sophisticated AI to examine employee performance. Supervised machine learning is applied to examine data from reviews, projects, and skill ratings to identify patterns in what causes high performance or points to improvement. The system attempts to eliminate bias in performance grades by applying data-driven insights rather than opinion-driven decisions, ensuring fairness.

It is also capable of identifying skill gaps and suggesting individual training, supporting continuous professional growth. It basically allows organizations to preemptively and more efficiently deal with performance and develop talent based on data. This application signifies a move toward proactive personnel development tactics and data-driven performance management (Fig. 9.1).

9.1.5 Culture Amp

Analyzes feedback, determined by AI, to facilitate keeping employees and addressing workplace problems. Culture Amp leverages AI in the form of text analysis and sentiment analysis to analyze and draw insights from employee feedback surveys and qualitative feedback. Algorithms used are able to detect emerging themes, shifts in sentiment, and drivers of employee satisfaction and dissatisfaction at scale.

9.1.6 Gloat

Forecasts employee turnover and performance catena, cueing HR for proactive interventions. Gloat relies mainly on sophisticated predictive analytics and machine learning. It pulls in and processes large volumes of internal HR data (e.g., pay, promotion history, tenure, and performance ratings) and some external data (e.g., economic data and industry standards).

The AI finds deep correlations and relationships in such data to forecast which employees will be most likely to leave the company (turnover) and forecast

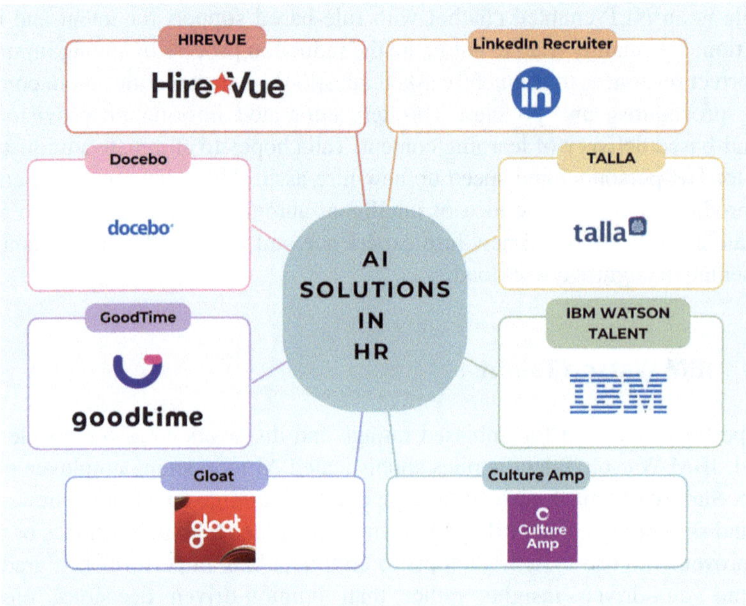

Fig. 9.1 Case studies on AI solutions in HR

individual or team performance trends. It is not a case of raw metrics; the AI can find the hidden relationships that elude human analysts. By getting ahead of turnover, HR is able to intervene in advance with at-risk employees.

9.1.7 GoodTime

Automatically schedules interviews, improving the candidate experience and eliminating scheduling issues. GoodTime applies natural language processing (NLP) to convert scheduling requests and limitations and optimization code to select the optimal interview times. This produces a positive impression about the firm.

9.1.8 Docebo

Delivers personalized training experiences according to the needs of the employee. Docebo's platform leverages machine learning as it studies the input from individual employees, such as their job function, skills, performance metrics, learning history, self-described career objectives, and even how they interact with the learning system itself (e.g., course completion, time spent, and search terms). It more than often uses natural language processing to decipher course content and compare it to skill gaps. Transitions from an entire-catalog training approach to a tightly targeted, context-specific learning approach, leading to more effective skill development.

Employees will be more inclined to engage with learning content that they perceive as being directly applicable to their life and work, as well as their professional career. Facilitates organizations to project and address gaps in the skills of the organization, enabling them to possess the skills needed for upcoming strategic initiatives. Through maximizing individualized, effective learning, there is greater utilization of assets, possibly cutting back on wasted time and financial resources on ineffective training. Encourages ongoing learning by bringing development opportunities within easy reach and highly applicable to one's context.

9.1.9 Entelo Diversity

Evaluates diversity and inclusion data for fairer hiring practices. Entelo Diversity utilizes AI, such as machine learning and possibly natural language processing, to survey enormous amounts of data on diversity and inclusion (D&I) in the recruitment and talent pipeline. These can encompass anonymized candidate information, employee demographics, patterns of hiring, and occasionally even job posting wording.

The AI assists organizations in finding out the demographic composition of their employees and candidates. It can detect potential hiring, screening, or sourcing biases by contrasting D&I metrics with benchmarks or targets.

It could, for instance, indicate whether a specific group is absent at a point in the hiring pipeline or if the job ads unintentionally discriminate against specific groups.

It anonymizes data, usually in order to maintain privacy, but keeps insights anyway. Provides accurate, actionable data to inform and complement diversity and inclusion initiatives instead of assumptions. Allows one to recognize and identify unconscious bias in the recruiting and talent management process to facilitate better and more equitable results. Through the identification of diversity gaps at the top of the funnel, HR may be able to change sourcing strategies to source a wider and more diversified candidate base.

Illustrates a focus on D&I, which becomes more and more valuable as a means of attracting and retaining top talent, particularly from historically underrepresented groups. Assists with D&I reporting needs and can assist in compliance with equal opportunity laws.

Together, AI offers avenues like machine learning, NLP, and predictive analysis, which are rendering HR functions more data-driven and efficient in industries. Figure 9.2 illustrates how various AI tools facilitate various HR functions, their roles, the technologies utilized, and the advantages.

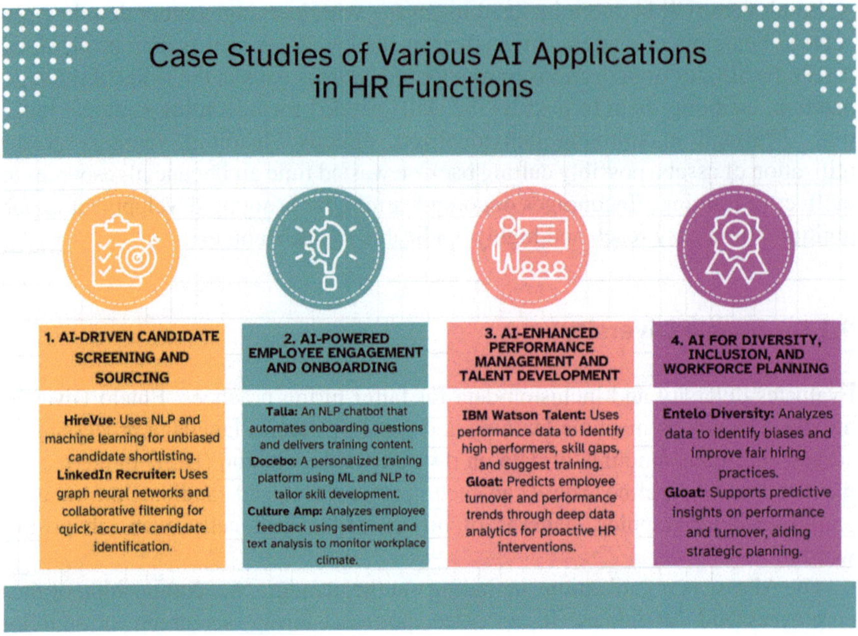

Fig. 9.2 Case study of various AI applications in HR functions

9.2 Case Studies on AI Solutions in HR and Alignment with the Monograph Results

The emergence of AI technologies and their exponential spread have led to a radical reorientation of corporate governance, especially as it relates to human resource management (HRM). As the case studies HireVue, LinkedIn Recruiter, Talla, IBM Watson Talent, Culture Amp, Gloat, GoodTime, Docebo, and Entelo Diversity demonstrate, insights stemming from AI are becoming an integral part of HR processes, making them more efficient, objective, tailored, and strategic. These operational implementations validate EMOMs as the growing organizational models that would align with the emergent models denoted by the agility, employee-centricity, digital integration, and ethical governance, and relate to the themes identified in the SLR and the affinity diagram.

9.2.1 AI-Powered HR Transformation and Employee-Focused Governance

The examples illustrate how companies are using AI to drive personalized employee development and experiences, a key theme of AI-powered HR transformation, and are in line with the first such tenet. For instance, being able to shortlist candidates quickly and without the introduction of bias is achieved with HireVue's machine learning and NLP features, which foster fair and unbiased recruiting. Likewise, Docebo's learning platforms customize personalized learning to suit your needs and promote ongoing skill growth. These are the solutions redefining HR regardless of your industry or company size, and moving from the old HR to employee-focused solutions that prioritize personalized growth paths and engagement. This change is reinforced with the monograph's conclusion, based on the observation that AI promotes collaboration and open communication, while it also enables job crafting and role redefinition, thus leading to a more adaptive and agile HR environment.

Shared occupational identity and AI engagement can add value, as the monograph suggests, which resonates with the use of virtual assistants (e.g., Talla) that foster team collaboration and accelerate onboarding. The focus on fairness and transparency in AI systems (Robert et al., 2020; Holmström & Carroll, 2024) reflects concerns in our case studies about building ethical AI that decreases bias and builds trust. By leveraging AI capabilities within HR processes, organizations promote a cultural change toward a more inclusive, participatory system of governance, which has been found to be crucial for the maintenance of organizational change in literature.

9.2.2 Governance Agility and Adaptability

The examples show how AI supports flexible and distributed governance structures in organizations. For example, Gloat's predictive analytics around who is leaving and who is performing well support proactive HR interventions, and that is consistent with the theme of agility in this monograph. Likewise, the automated interview scheduling of GoodTime lessens the admin load, freeing HR up to concentrate on higher-value strategic tasks. AI's ability to distribute decision rights and prompt a faster response to external shifts also enables the introduction of flatter organizational structures like that of holacracy.

These cases lend empirical support to literature perspectives on agile governance (defined here by flexible architectures, decentralized decision-making, and innovation cultures). Organizations are trending toward more dynamic roles, and management is becoming more decentralized (Jatobá et al., 2023).

Organizations are adopting AI-enabled forms of governance to facilitate rapid adaptation to volatile markets. AI's ability to deal with real-time data and drive decision-making supports organizational resiliency, in line with the monograph messaging around cultivating a culture of continuous learning and innovation.

9.2.3 Integration of Digital Technologies and Organizational Performance

The case studies' use of "AI tools" as IBM Watson Talent and Entelo Diversity demonstrate the degree and level of digital integration, which will improve organizational effectiveness through the use of data-driven decisions congruent with strategy. They contribute to the theme of how AI is used to optimize organizational performance with tools in the form of capability to perfect objective performance measures, assess diversity metrics, and plan strategically. The use of AI for governance applications, such as for change management frameworks, enhances organizations' capability to successfully maneuver through complex transformations.

The empirical evidences in the case studies show the significance of being technologically prepared, strategically investing in infrastructure (Sandkuhl, 2019; Neumann et al., 2024). Indeed, the crafting of AI-compatible systems by organizations constitutes proactive change management and reflects extant literature stressing the need for strong leadership support and cross-functional coordination to incorporate AI into organizational routines.

9.2.4 Leadership and Culture Transformation: Accelerator with AI

Transformational leadership models are critical for helping organizations navigate the changes resulting from AI, a fact evident in the focus of the case studies on AI-enhanced leadership insights and decision-making. AI analytical leaders can create an environment in which innovation, motivation, and change are welcomed (Mouazen et al., 2024). The application of AI on monitoring team dynamics and team performance (Nie, 2024) supplements the transformational leadership, allowing for leverage more informed and adaptive approach.

There is also the historical dimension, which, as the [monograph] shows, shows the need for a supportive, experiential environment. AI serves to underpin this process by providing ongoing revisioning and learning support, as well as a willingness for companies to take risks (Gendron et al., 2024). By building an AI-friendly culture, engaging staff in innovation processes, and confronting pushback, organizations can be better-suited to making the most of what AI has to offer in the realm of governance.

9.2.5 Data-Informed HRM and Strategy Linking

The rise of data-driven HR practices (e.g., AI-driven performance systems (Mikalef et al., 2023) is consistent with the theme of strategic alignment found in this monograph. The cases demonstrate how AI supports the development of real-time decision-making and intelligence through hyper-personalized talent management and interventions, building a culture of accountability and transparency.

Effective change governance is also about embedding AI into existing models, like Kotter's model for an easier transition (Nie, 2024). The examples' emphasis on AI as an agent of change (by interpreting and responding to constant feedback and providing a picture of future scenarios) supports the literature claims related to AI support for agile and resilient organizations.

9.2.6 AI Culture, Ethics, and Responsibility

Lastly, this monograph highlights the significance of ethical, responsible AI governance, a focus that is evident in the case studies in terms of fairness, transparency, and the involvement of relevant stakeholders. There is growing awareness among organizations that AI adoption should be guided by ethical concerns such as algorithmic bias, data privacy, and environmental sustainability (Venugopal et al., 2024; Jatobá et al., 2023). Setting ethical governance measures in place is crucial to ensure AI is trustworthy and to gain societal acceptance—a requirement for long-term success.

The culture change required for AI adoption was a mixture of promoting collaboration, the ability to always learn, and openness (those are all ingredients for good AI). The emphasis on responsible AI governance, then, supports the monograph's discussion of the intertwining of sustainability and ethical practices in organizational change management as organizations navigate societal expectations and the regulatory environment.

The alignment of CS data and scholarly insights points to a new era in corporate governance, that of a paradigm shift from rigid HR models to ethically grounded, AI-empowered, and dynamic frameworks. Applied-AI case studies demonstrate the ways that organizations are nurturing agility, personalization, and strategy to support the monograph's overarching narratives of adaptive governance, cultural change, and ethical responsibility.

9.3 Public, Private, and Tech vs. Non-Tech Implementations

AI governance in the public sector serves public interest, justice, and citizens' rights more, depending on strong regulation such as GDPR, with a focus on bias avoidance and due process. AI social welfare fraud detection (e.g., USA and UK), for instance, involves open decision-making and appeal processes to avoid wrongful denial and biased algorithms impacting vulnerable populations (Taeihagh, 2025). In the same vein, predictive policing seeks to prevent crime without AI replicating historical biases, as the White House's Blueprint for an AI Bill of Rights underscores. Public health surveillance, such as WHO activities, concentrates on data privacy, consent, and fair utilization of AI outcomes (WHO news, March 2025).

On the other hand, regulation of AI by private industry is driven by profitability and innovation and moderates these with legal, reputational, and ethical risk. For the financial sector, AI for credit and fraud management targets model risk management and compliance (McKinsey, March 2025; WEF report, 2025). E-commerce employs AI for customized recommendations and targets data privacy and fair practice as measures to reduce reputational risk. For autonomous vehicles, the law is focusing on safety, accountability, and ethical decision-making, and it requires extensive testing and regulation (arXiv paper, "Kulothungan & Gupta," May 2025).

Technology vs. Non-Technology Organization AI Governance

Tech companies such as Google and OpenAI lead the development of AI and fall under tremendous scrutiny. Regulation for them includes in-house ethics committees, principles-based approaches (e.g., Google AI Principles), and substantive investment in Responsible AI research. When it comes to Large Language Models (LLMs), regulation comprises intellectual property and demands ongoing monitoring and safety guardrails (Oxford Academic, Policy and Society, Feb 2025). Cloud-based AI services commit to the safe and ethical provision of tools, whereas social media companies address fake news and algorithmic amplification of hateful content through complex policy formulation.

Non-tech firms (e.g., manufacturing and healthcare) use AI for the most part for consumption. Their own leadership implements approved risk norms with emphasis on vendor due diligence, impact assessment, and employee training. In healthcare, diagnostic AI is heavily regulated by patient safety and data privacy (HIPAA), with cross-functional governance necessary to manage potential bias (Forbes Tech Council, Jan 2025). Manufacturing applies AI for predictive maintenance, where governance ensures safe operation, data security, and upskilling of employees (Baxter, April 2025). Agriculture depends on precision farming with AI addressing questions of data ownership and fair access to technology.

Public sector and non-tech organizations prefer risk-averse, compliance-driven AI governance prioritizing social effect, while private sector and tech organizations, though gradually regulated and subject to public pressure, seek competitive advantage and innovation (Fig. 9.3).

This monograph examines the change in paradigm in organizational governance prompted by rapid technological advancements and the complex, uncertain nature of the VUCA world of today. It provides the transition from classical, control-oriented HR models to emerging, innovative AI-based governance models that emphasize agility, employee-centric practices, data-driven decision-making, and ethics. Through systematic literature review and analysis, this monograph identifies seven emerging organizational models that reflect governance in change. It offers practical case studies and leadership insights to support organizations adapt, survive, and lead proactively amid continuous turbulence, filling key research gaps and providing an inclusive guide for future governance in an AI-enabled world.

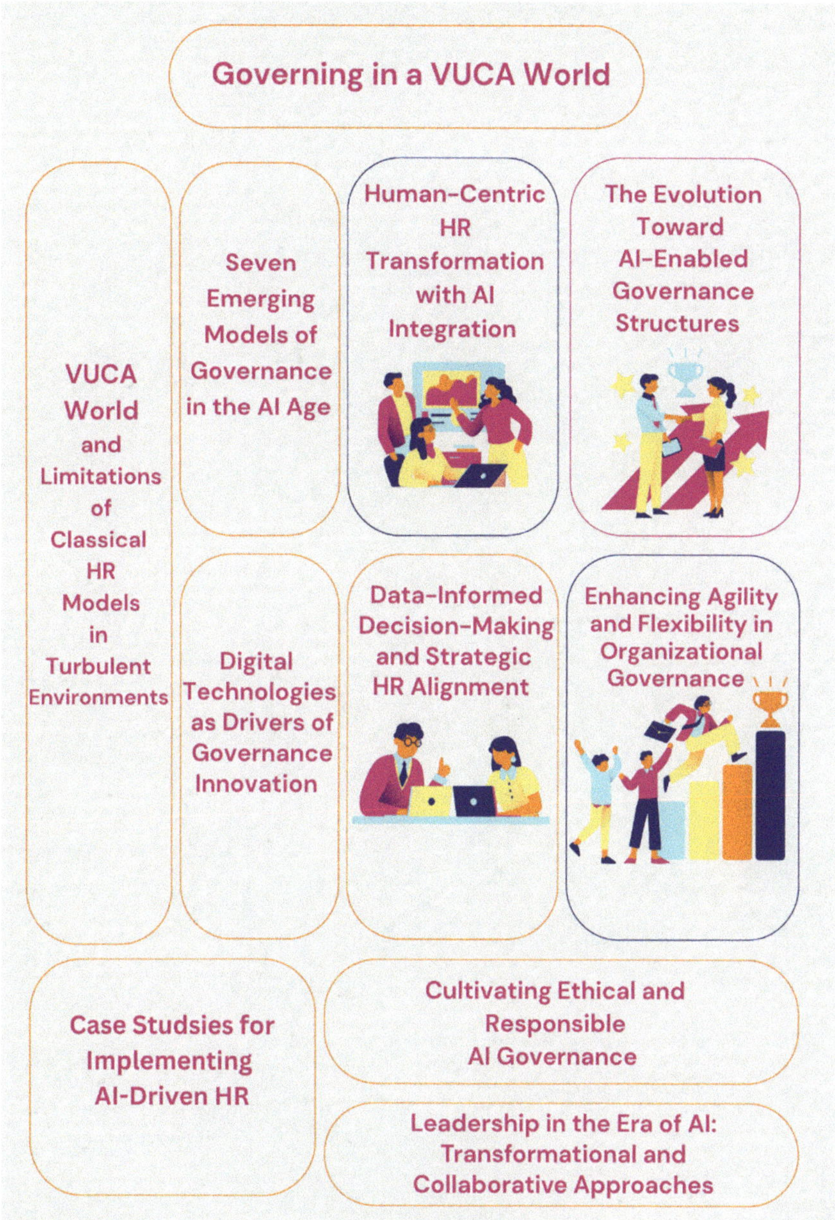

Fig. 9.3 Governing in change in AI age and innovative HR models

Glossary

Artificial Intelligence (AI) Refers to the simulation of human mental operations performed by machines, specifically computer systems.

Data-Driven Processes HR business decision-making and processes are based primarily on the interpretation and analysis of data and are often aided by AI tools for extracting insights more holistically.

Ethical AI AI system design and deployment such that they are guided by moral principles, are equitable across all, transparent, accountable, and respectful of human rights and welfare.

Job Crafting The way that workers voluntarily re-shape job tasks and duties in a fashion that better matches their capability, passion, and values may be enhanced in the current AI age by re-visioning human-AI collaborations.

Reskilling Acquiring new skills to do a new job or to cope with drastic changes to an existing job role, usually brought about by technological improvements such as AI.

SLR (Systematic Literature Review) A systematic and staged research technique employed to identify, assess, and synthesize all high-quality studies pertinent to a given research problem, usually in order to respond to a particular research question.

Talent Acquisition The task involves seeking out, attracting, evaluating, and appointing appropriate candidates to fulfill an organization's staffing needs.

Transformational Leadership A leadership approach where the leaders motivate and energize their subordinates to deliver exceptional results, generally by creating innovation, breaking routine standards, and fostering individual development, most applicable in AI implementation.

Upskilling The learning process of acquiring new skills or developing existing skills to improve performance in a current job position or to prepare oneself for future development is very much needed in an AI-based work environment.

A. Rosa, *New Business Organizational Models for Governing in Times of Change*, Future of Business and Finance,
https://doi.org/10.1007/978-3-032-04091-6

References

Agrawal, K. (2024). Towards adoption of generative AI in organizational settings. *Journal of Computer Information Systems, 64*(5), 636–651.

Alamri, J. M. (2025). Antecedents of generative artificial intelligence technology adoption: Extended innovation of diffusion model with cultural dimensions and risks perceptions. *Journal of Ecohumanism, 4*(1), 1718–1738.

Aldoseri, A., Al-Khalifa, K. N., & Hamouda, A. M. (2024). Methodological approach to assessing the current state of organizations for AI-based digital transformation. *Applied System Innovation, 7*(1), 14.

Ali Mohamad, T., Bastone, A., Bernhard, F., & Schiavone, F. (2023). How artificial intelligence impacts the competitive position of healthcare organizations. *Journal of Organizational Change Management, 36*(8), 49–70.

Alzeiby, E. A., Islam, N., Shaik, A. S., & Yaqub, M. Z. (2025). AI adoption in enterprises for enhanced strategic human resource management practices: Benefiting the employee engagement and experience. *Journal of Enterprise Information Management.* https://doi.org/10.1108/JEIM-05-2024-0249

Amoako, R., Jiang, Y., Frempong, M. F., Tetteh, S., & Adu-Yeboah, S. S. (2022). Examining the effect of organizational leadership, organizational structure, and employee technological capability on the success of electronic human resource management. *Sage Open, 12*(2), 21582440221088852.

Araz Taeihagh, Governance of Generative AI, Policy and Society, Volume 44, Issue 1, January 2025, Pages 1–22, https://doi.org/10.1093/polsoc/puaf001

Aria, M., & Cuccurullo, C. (2017). bibliometrix: An R-tool for comprehensive science mapping analysis. *Journal of Informetrics, 11*(4), 959–975.

Atanassova, I., Bednar, P., Khan, H., & Khan, Z. (2025). Managing the VUCA environment: The dynamic role of organizational learning and strategic agility in B2B versus B2C firms. *Industrial Marketing Management, 125*, 12–28.

Azzam, M., & Beckmann, R. (2022). How AI helps to increase organizations' capacity to manage complexity–a research perspective and solution approach bridging different disciplines. *IEEE Transactions on Engineering Management, 71*, 2324–2337.

Bagis, F., & Yulianeu, A. (2024). Enhancing employee performance through AI-enabled HR analytics: Exploring the roles of job crafting, perceived risk, and employee engagement. *Journal of Digitovation and information system, 4*(1), 81–97.

Bankins, S., Ocampo, A. C., Marrone, M., Restubog, S. L. D., & Woo, S. E. (2024). A multilevel review of artificial intelligence in organizations: Implications for organizational behavior research and practice. *Journal of Organizational Behavior, 45*(2), 159–182.

Baumann, O., & Wu, B. (2023). Managerial hierarchy in AI-driven organizations. *Journal of Organization Design, 12*(1), 1–5.

A. Rosa, *New Business Organizational Models for Governing in Times of Change*, Future of Business and Finance,
https://doi.org/10.1007/978-3-032-04091-6

Benbya, H., Davenport, T. H., & Pachidi, S. (2020). Artificial intelligence in organizations: Current state and future opportunities. *MIS Quarterly Executive, 19*(4).

Bennett, N., & Lemoine, G. J. (2014). What a difference a word makes: Understanding threats to performance in a VUCA world. *Business Horizons, 57*(3), 311–317.

Berente, N., Gu, B., Recker, J., & Santhanam, R. (2021). Managing artificial intelligence. *MIS quarterly, 45*(3).

Bonanomi, M. M., Hall, D. M., Staub-French, S., Tucker, A., & Talamo, C. M. L. (2020). The impact of digital transformation on formal and informal organizational structures of large architecture and engineering firms. *Engineering, Construction and Architectural Management, 27*(4), 872–892.

Booth, A. (2016). Searching for qualitative research for inclusion in systematic reviews: A structured methodological review. *Systematic Reviews, 5*(1), 74.

Brink, A., Benyayer, L. D., & Kupp, M. (2024). Decision-making in organizations: Should managers use AI? *Journal of Business Strategy, 45*(4), 267–274.

Cao, G., Duan, Y., Edwards, J. S., & Dwivedi, Y. K. (2021). Understanding managers' attitudes and behavioral intentions towards using artificial intelligence for organizational decision-making. *Technovation, 106*, 102312.

Carayannis, E. G., Papamichail, G., Zotas, N., et al. (2025). Corporate foresight: Navigating uncertainty in a VUCA world. *Journal of the Knowledge Economy*. https://doi.org/10.1007/s13132-024-02587-4

Chiu, Y. T., Zhu, Y. Q., & Corbett, J. (2021). In the hearts and minds of employees: A model of pre-adoptive appraisal toward artificial intelligence in organizations. *International Journal of Information Management, 60*, 102379.

Cochrane Qualitative and Implementation Methods Group. (2020). *Guidance for conducting qualitative evidence synthesis*. APA Journal Article Reporting Standards (JARS) for qualitative research.

Cole, M. D. (2024). AI regulation and governance on a global scale: An overview of international, regional and national instruments. *Journal of AI Law and Regulation, 1*(1), 126–142.

Collis, J., & Hussey, R. (2014). Writing up the Research. In Business research (pp. 297–330). Palgrave, London.

Cummings, S., Bridgman, T., & Brown, K. G. (2016). Unfreezing change as three steps: Rethinking Kurt Lewin's legacy for change management. *Human Relations, 69*(1), 33–60.

Curtis, C., Gillespie, N., & Lockey, S. (2023). AI-deploying organizations are key to addressing 'perfect storm' of AI risks. *AI Ethics, 3*, 145–153. https://doi.org/10.1007/s43681-022-00163-7

De Cremer, D., & Narayanan, D. (2023). How AI tools can—and cannot—help organizations become more ethical. *Frontiers in Artificial Intelligence, 6*, 1093712.

DiRomualdo, A., El-Khoury, D., & Girimonte, F. (2018). HR in the digital age: How digital technology will change HR's organization structure, processes and roles. *Strategic HR Review, 17*(5), 234–242.

Divya, D., Jain, R., Chetty, P., Siwach, V., & Mathur, A. (2024). The mediating effect of leadership in artificial intelligence success for employee-engagement. *Management Decision*. https://doi.org/10.1108/MD-01-2024-0213

Douglas, S., & Haley, G. R. (2025). Transforming HR into a strategic partner: A case study of organizational redesign for sustainable growth. *Strategic HR Review*. https://doi.org/10.1108/SHR-12-2024-0101

Elkahlout, M., Karaja, M. B., Elsharif, A. A., Dheir, I. M., Abunasser, B. S., & Abu-Naser, S. S. (2024). AI-driven organizational change: Transforming structures and processes in the modern workplace. *International Journal of Academic Information Systems Research, 8*, 24–28.

Esmaeilzadeh, P. (2024). Challenges and strategies for wide-scale artificial intelligence (AI) deployment in healthcare practices: A perspective for healthcare organizations. *Artificial Intelligence in Medicine, 151*, 102861.

Fatmawati, E., Suharto, B., Amrozi, S. R., Suhma, W. K., Yudiawan, A., Ilyasin, M., & Suhma, F. M. (2024). Change management towards good university governance in Indonesia: Study at Islamic religious universities based on BLU mandate. *Cogent Social Sciences, 10*(1), 2333081.

Fioravante, R., & Vaccaro, A. (2024). Personalism in generative AI deployment: Deciding ethically when human creative expression is at stake. *Humanistic Management Journal*. https://doi.org/10.1007/s41463-024-00193-9

Gendron, Y., Andrew, J., Cooper, C., & Tregidga, H. (2024). On the juggernaut of artificial intelligence in organizations, research and society. *Critical Perspectives on Accounting, 102759.*

Gladden, M., Fortuna, P., & Modliński, A. (2022). The empowerment of artificial intelligence in post-digital organizations: Exploring human interactions with supervisory AI. *Human Technology, 18*(2), 98–121.

Gursoy, D., & Cai, R. (2025). Artificial intelligence: An overview of research trends and future directions. *International Journal of Contemporary Hospitality Management, 37*(1), 1–17.

Hannes, K., & Macaitis, K. (2012). Critical appraisal of qualitative research: A review of the literature. *International Journal of Evidence-Based Healthcare, 10*(1), 47–71.

Herrmann, T., & Pfeiffer, S. (2023). Keeping the organization in the loop: A socio-technical extension of human-centered artificial intelligence. *AI & Society, 38*(4), 1523–1542.

Holmström, J., & Carroll, N. (2024). How organizations can innovate with generative AI. *Business Horizons, 68*(5), 559–573.

https://www.who.int/europe/news/item/10-03-2025-who-announces-new-collaborating-centre-on-ai-for-healthgovernance#:~:text=The%20World%20Health%20Organization%20%28WHO%29%20today%20designated%20the,care%2C%20save%20lives%20and%20improve%20health%20and%20well-being.

https://www.forbes.com/sites/jasonsnyder/2025/01/19/beyond-the-illusionthe-real-threat-of-ai-wef-global-risks-report-2025/

https://www.forbes.com/sites/forbeseq/2025/09/30/the-aging-and-disability-crisis-we-cant-afford-to-ignore/

https://www.mckinsey.com/capabilities/mckinsey-digital/our-insights/superagency-in-the-workplace-empowering-people-to-unlock-ais-full-potential-at-work

https://www.techmarketview.com/news/archive/2025/04/09/ukhotviewsextra-oneadvanced-launches-sovereign-ai-service

Hradecky, D., Kennell, J., Cai, W., & Davidson, R. (2022). Organizational readiness to adopt artificial intelligence in the exhibition sector in Western Europe. *International Journal of Information Management, 65*, 102497.

Ijaiya, H., & Odumuwagun, O. O. (2024). Advancing artificial intelligence and safeguarding data privacy: A comparative study of EU and US regulatory frameworks amid emerging cyber threats. *International Journal of Research Publication and Reviews, 5*(12), 3357–3375.

Iqbal, S., Ashfaq, T., & Taib, C. A. B. (2022). A systematic literature review on organizational performance in global higher education: An affinity diagram approach. *Pakistan Journal of Social Research, 4*(1), 688–701.

Islam, R. (2005). Prioritization of ideas in an affinity diagram by the AHP: An example of k-economy. *International Journal of Economics, Management and Accounting, 13.*

Islam, M. M., & Shuford, J. (2024). A survey of ethical considerations in AI: Navigating the landscape of bias and fairness. *Journal of Artificial Intelligence General Science (JAIGS), 1*(1).

Jarrahi, M. H., Kenyon, S., Brown, A., Donahue, C., & Wicher, C. (2023). Artificial intelligence: A strategy to harness its power through organizational learning. *Journal of Business Strategy, 44*(3), 126–135.

Jatobá, M. N., Ferreira, J. J., Fernandes, P. O., & Teixeira, J. P. (2023). Intelligent human resources for the adoption of artificial intelligence: A systematic literature review. *Journal of Organizational Change Management, 36*(7), 1099–1124.

John, B., Alsamarra'i, Z., & Panteli, N. (2024). Reconfiguring digital embeddedness in hybrid work: The case of employee experience management platforms. *Information Systems Journal, 35*(2), 450–479.

Jöhnk, J., Weißert, M., & Wyrtki, K. (2021). Ready or not, AI comes—an interview study of organizational AI readiness factors. *Business & Information Systems Engineering, 63*(1), 5–20.

Joseph, G. (2025). Embracing resilience in pharmaceutical manufacturing: "Digital twins"–forging a resilient path in the VUCA maze. *International Journal of Pharmaceutical and Healthcare Marketing*. https://doi.org/10.1108/IJPHM-03-2024-0024

Joseph, J., & Sengul, M. (2025). Organization design: Current insights and future research directions. *Journal of Management, 51*(1), 249–308.

Kaur, M., Rekha, A. G., & Vikas, S. (2021). Adoption of artificial intelligence in human resource management. *Indian Journal of Industrial Relations, 57*(2), 331–342.

Khushk, A., Zhiying, L., Yi, X., & Aman, N. (2025). AI-driven HR transformation in Chinese automotive industry: Strategies and implications. *Business Process Management Journal*. https://doi.org/10.1108/BPMJ-11-2023-0915

Kolbjørnsrud, V., Amico, R., & Thomas, R. J. (2017). Partnering with AI: How organizations can win over skeptical managers. *Strategy & Leadership, 45*(1), 37–43. https://doi.org/10.1108/SL-12-2016-0085

Kulothungan, V., & Gupta, D. (2025, May). Towards adaptive AI governance: Comparative insights from the US, EU, and Asia. In 2025 IEEE 11th Conference on Big Data Security on Cloud (BigDataSecurity) (pp. 32–38). IEEE.

Kulshrestha, S. (2024). Quantitative assessment on investigation on the impact of artificial intelligence on HR practices and organizational efficiency for Industry 4.0. *Journal of Artificial Intelligence Machine Learning and Neural Network, 4*(42), 14–21.

Kurup, S., & Gupta, V. (2022). Factors influencing the AI adoption in organizations. *Metamorphosis, 21*(2), 129–139.

Landis, J. R., & Koch, G. G. (1977). The measurement of observer agreement for categorical data. *Biometrics, 33*, 159–174.

Lee, M. C., Scheepers, H., Lui, A. K., & Ngai, E. W. (2023). The implementation of artificial intelligence in organizations: A systematic literature review. *Information and Management, 60*(5), 103816.

Lemos, S. I., Ferreira, F. A., Zopounidis, C., Galariotis, E., & Ferreira, N. C. (2022). Artificial intelligence and change management in small and medium-sized enterprises: An analysis of dynamics within adaptation initiatives. *Annals of Operations Research*, 1–27. https://doi.org/10.1007/s10479-022-05159-4

Lewandowski, T., Delling, J., Grotherr, C., & Böhmann, T. (2021). State-of-the-art analysis of adopting AI-based conversational agents in organizations: A systematic literature review. *PACIS, 167*.

Li, J., & Yeo, R. K. (2024). Artificial intelligence and human integration: A conceptual exploration of its influence on work processes and workplace learning. *Human Resource Development International, 27*(3), 367–387. https://doi.org/10.1080/13678868.2024.2348987

Madanchian, M., & Taherdoost, H. (2025). Barriers and enablers of AI adoption in human resource management: A critical analysis of organizational and technological factors. *Information, 16*(1), 51.

Mahboub, R., & Ghanem, M. G. (2024). The mediating role of knowledge management practices and balanced scorecard in the association between artificial intelligence and organization performance: Evidence from MENA region commercial banks. *Cogent Business & Management, 11*(1), 2404484.

Maragno, G., Tangi, L., Gastaldi, L., & Benedetti, M. (2023). Exploring the factors, affordances and constraints outlining the implementation of Artificial Intelligence in public sector organizations. *International Journal of Information Management, 73*, 102686.

Massaro, M., Dumay, J., & Guthrie, J. (2016). On the shoulders of giants: Undertaking a structured literature review in accounting. *Accounting, Auditing & Accountability Journal, 29*(5), 767–801.

Miao, Q., & Nduneseokwu, C. (2024). Applications of leadership theories and concepts in environmental leadership. In *Environmental Leadership in a VUCA Era*. Springer. https://doi.org/10.1007/978-981-96-0324-4_6

Mikalef, P., Lemmer, K., Schaefer, C., Ylinen, M., Fjørtoft, S. O., Torvatn, H. Y., et al. (2023). Examining how AI capabilities can foster organizational performance in public organizations. *Government Information Quarterly, 40*(2), 101797.

Mirdasse, S. (2024). Digitalization and performance management: A conceptual framework for HR governance. *Journal of Economics, Finance and Management (JEFM), 3*(3), 642–664.

Mirsky, Y., Demontis, A., Kotak, J., Shankar, R., Gelei, D., Yang, L., et al. (2023). The threat of offensive ai to organizations. *Computers & Security, 124*, 103006.

Misra, S. K., Sharma, S. K., Gupta, S., & Das, S. (2023). A framework to overcome challenges to the adoption of artificial intelligence in Indian government organizations. *Technological Forecasting and Social Change, 194*, 122721.

Moher, D., Liberati, A., Tetzlaff, J., Altman, D. G., & The PRISMA Group. (2009). Preferred Reporting Items for Systematic Reviews and Meta Analyses: The PRISMA Statement. *PLoS Med., 6*(6), e1000097. https://doi.org/10.1371/journal.pmed1000097

Montero Guerra, J. M., & Danvila-Del Valle, I. (2024). Exploring organizational change in the age of digital transformation and its impact on talent management: Trends and challenges. *Journal of Organizational Change Management, 37*(6), 1273–1294.

Mouazen, A. M., Hernández-Lara, A. B., Abdallah, F., Ramadan, M., Chahine, J., Baydoun, H., & Bou Zakhem, N. (2024). Transformational and transactional leaders and their role in implementing the Kotter change management model ensuring sustainable change: An empirical study. *Sustainability, 16*(1), 16.

Neumann, O., Guirguis, K., & Steiner, R. (2024). Exploring artificial intelligence adoption in public organizations: A comparative case study. *Public Management Review, 26*(1), 114–141.

Nie, Q. (2024). Application of artificial intelligence in enterprise human resource management and employee performance evaluation. *International Journal of Computer Applications in Technology, 74*(3), 186–196.

Olan, F., Arakpogun, E. O., Suklan, J., Nakpodia, F., Damij, N., & Jayawickrama, U. (2022). Artificial intelligence and knowledge sharing: Contributing factors to organizational performance. *Journal of Business Research, 145*, 605–615.

Olsson, A. K., Eriksson, K. M., & Carlsson, L. (2025). Management toward Industry 5.0: A co-workership approach on digital transformation for future innovative manufacturing. *European Journal of Innovation Management, 28*(1), 65–84. https://doi.org/10.1108/EJIM-09-2023-0833

Ooi, K. B., Tan, G. W. H., Al-Emran, M., Al-Sharafi, M. A., Capatina, A., Chakraborty, A., et al. (2023). The potential of generative artificial intelligence across disciplines: Perspectives and future directions. *Journal of Computer Information Systems, 65*, 76–107.

Ötting, S. K., Masjutin, L., & Maier, G. W. (2021). The future of leadership—How is leadership in small and medium-sized enterprises going to change? *Gruppe. Interaktion. Organisation. Zeitschrift für Angewandte Organisationspsychologie (GIO), 52*(4), 639–647.

Papagiannidis, E., Mikalef, P., & Conboy, K. (2025). Responsible artificial intelligence governance: A review and research framework. *The Journal of Strategic Information Systems, 34*(2), 101885.

Perez, F., Conway, N., & Roques, O. (2022). The autonomy tussle: AI technology and employee job crafting responses. *Relations industrielles/Industrial Relations, 77*(3).

Piercy, N., Phillips, W., & Lewis, M. (2013). Change management in the public sector: The use of cross-functional teams. *Production Planning & Control, 24*(10-11), 976–987.

Pillai, R., & Sivathanu, B. (2020). Adoption of artificial intelligence (AI) for talent acquisition in IT/ITeS organizations. *Benchmarking: An International Journal, 27*(9), 2599–2629.

Popli, S., & Rizvi, I. A. (2016). Drivers of employee engagement: The role of leadership style. *Global Business Review, 17*(4), 965–979.

Prasad Agrawal, K. (2024). Towards adoption of generative AI in organizational settings. *Journal of Computer Information Systems, 64*(5), 636–651.

Raisch, S., & Fomina, K. (2023). Combining human and artificial intelligence: Hybrid problem-solving in organizations. *Academy of Management Review*. https://doi.org/10.5465/amr.2021.0421

Raisch, S., & Krakowski, S. (2021). Artificial intelligence and management: The automation–augmentation paradox. *Academy of management review, 46*(1), 192–210.

Robert, L. P., Pierce, C., Marquis, L., Kim, S., & Alahmad, R. (2020). Designing fair AI for managing employees in organizations: A review, critique, and design agenda. *Human–Computer Interaction, 35*(5-6), 545–575.

Rožman, M., Tominc, P., & Milfelner, B. (2023). Maximizing employee engagement through artificial intelligent organizational culture in the context of leadership and training of employees: Testing linear and non-linear relationships. *Cogent Business & Management, 10*(2), 2248732.

Rudko, I., Bashirpour Bonab, A., Fedele, M., & Formisano, A. V. (2024). New institutional theory and AI: Toward rethinking of artificial intelligence in organizations. *Journal of Management History, 31*, 261–284.

Samir, M. I. R. D. A. S. S. E. (2024). Digitalization and Performance Management: A Conceptual Framework for HR Governance. *Journal of Economics, Finance and Management (JEFM), 3*(3), 642–664.

Sandelowski, M. (2006). The impact of qualitative research on evidence-based practice. *Research in Nursing & Health, 29*(1), 88–96.

Sandelowski, M., Sandelowski, M. J., & Barroso, J. (2006). Handbook for synthesizing qualitative research. Springer publishing company.

Sandkuhl, K. (2019, July). Putting AI into context-method support for the introduction of artificial intelligence into organizations. In *2019 IEEE 21st Conference on Business Informatics (CBI)* (Vol. 1, pp. 157-164). IEEE.

Sarioguz, O., & Miser, E. (2024). Artificial intelligence and participatory leadership: The role of technological transformation in business management and its impact on employee participation. *International Research Journal of Modernization in Engineering, Technology and Science, 6*(2).

Schaefer, S. M., & Alvesson, M. (2020). Epistemic attitudes and source critique in qualitative research. *Journal of Management Inquiry, 29*(1), 33–45.

Shick, M., Johnson, N., & Fan, Y. (2024). Artificial intelligence and the end of bounded rationality: A new era in organizational decision making. *Development and Learning in Organizations: An International Journal, 38*(4), 1–3.

Shrestha, Y. R., Ben-Menahem, S. M., & Von Krogh, G. (2019). Organizational decision-making structures in the age of artificial intelligence. *California Management Review, 61*(4), 66–83.

Simón, C., Revilla, E., & Sáenz, M. J. (2024). Integrating AI in organizations for value creation through human-AI teaming: A dynamic-capabilities approach. *Journal of Business Research, 182*, 114783.

Singhraul, B. P., & Anuragi, D. (2024). Human resource management in the digital era. *International Journal of Research in Commerce and Management Studies*. https://doi.org/10.38193/IJRCMS.2024.6515

Smith, M., Prabhakar, G., Nisar, T. M., & Tseng, H. T. (2024). Adoption of AI by the HR function in the civil service. *Employee Relations: The International Journal, 47*, 104–126.

Snyder, H. (2019). Literature review as a research methodology: An overview and guidelines. *Journal of Business Research, 104*, 333–339.

Ştefan, S. C., Olariu, A. A., & Popa, S. C. (2024). Implications of artificial intelligence on organizational agility: A PLS-SEM and PLS-POS approach. *Amfiteatru Economic, 26*(66), 403–420.

Storbacka, K., & Nenonen, S. (2009). Customer relationships and the heterogeneity of firm performance. *Journal of Business & Industrial Marketing, 24*(5/6), 360–372.

Stouten, J., Rousseau, D. M., & De Cremer, D. (2018). Successful organizational change: Integrating the management practice and scholarly literatures. *Academy of Management Annals, 12*(2), 752–788.

Tambe, P., Cappelli, P., & Yakubovich, V. (2019). Artificial intelligence in human resources management: Challenges and a path forward. *California Management Review, 61*(4), 15–42.

Taskan, B., Junça-Silva, A., & Caetano, A. (2022). Clarifying the conceptual map of VUCA: A systematic review. *International Journal of Organizational Analysis, 30*(7), 196–217. https://doi.org/10.1108/IJOA-02-2022-3136

Thomas, J., & Harden, A. (2008). Methods for the thematic synthesis of qualitative research in systematic reviews. *BMC Medical Research Methodology, 8*(1), 45.

Tims, M., Bakker, A. B., Derks, D., & Van Rhenen, W. (2013). Job crafting at the team and individual level: Implications for work engagement and performance. *Group & Organization Management, 38*(4), 427–454.

Tohănean, D., Buzatu, A. I., Baba, C. A., & Georgescu, B. (2020). Business model innovation through the use of digital technologies: Managing risks and creating sustainability. *Amfiteatru Economic, 22*(55), 758–774.

Top 15 Real-Life Use Cases For AI In the Human Resources Industry. (n.d.). https://redresscompliance.com/top-15-real-life-use-cases-for-ai-in-the-human-resources-industry/

Trunk, A., Birkel, H., & Hartmann, E. (2020). On the current state of combining human and artificial intelligence for strategic organizational decision making. *Business Research, 13*(3), 875–919.

Venugopal, M., Madhavan, V., Prasad, R., & Raman, R. (2024). Transformative AI in human resource management: enhancing workforce planning with topic modeling. *Cogent Business & Management, 11*(1), 2432550.

Wang, H., & Guo, J. (2024). New way out of efficiency-equity dilemma: Digital technology empowerment for local government environmental governance. *Technological Forecasting and Social Change, 200*, 123184.

Winchester, C. L., & Salji, M. (2016). Writing a literature review. *Journal of Clinical Urology, 9*(5), 308–312.

Wrzesniewski, A., & Dutton, J. E. (2001). Crafting a job: Revisioning employees as active crafters of their work. *Academy of Management Review, 26*(2), 179–201.

Xiao, Q., Yan, J., & Bamber, G. J. (2025). How does AI-enabled HR analytics influence employee resilience: Job crafting as a mediator and HRM system strength as a moderator. *Personnel Review, 54*(3), 824–843.

Zharova, A. K. (2023). Achieving algorithmic transparency and managing risks of data security when making decisions without human interference: Legal approaches. *Journal of Digital Technologies and Law, 1*(4), 973–993.

Zheng, D. (2024). Key factors in organizational change: Case studies of Netflix and FinoTechno using change management models. *Advances in Economics, Management and Political Sciences, 113*, 1–8.

MIX
Papier aus verantwortungsvollen Quellen
Paper from responsible sources
FSC® C105338

If you have any concerns about our products,
you can contact us on
ProductSafety@springernature.com

In case Publisher is established outside the EU,
the EU authorized representative is:
Springer Nature Customer Service Center GmbH
Europaplatz 3, 69115 Heidelberg, Germany

Printed by Libri Plureos GmbH
in Hamburg, Germany